Creativity for 21st Century Skills

Creativity for 21st Century Skills

How to Embed Creativity into the Curriculum

Jane Piirto
Ashland University, Ohio, USA

SENSE PUBLISHERS
ROTTERDAM/BOSTON/TAIPEI

A C.I.P. record for this book is available from the Library of Congress.

ISBN: 978-94-6091-461-4 (paperback)
ISBN: 978-94-6091-462-1 (hardback)
ISBN: 978-94-6091-463-8 (e-book)

Published by: Sense Publishers,
P.O. Box 21858,
3001 AW Rotterdam,
The Netherlands
www.sensepublishers.com

Printed on acid-free paper

DEDICATION

To Steven, Denise, and Danielle
(of course)

CONTENTS

PREFACE

I've been teaching since 1964, when I was a young mother and graduate assistant in the English department, while getting my first master's degree.

My take on creativity enhancement comes from a many-factored background that few who write in the education and psychology area have. I have been a teacher, an education and English professor, a school and college administrator for all levels, from pre-K through doctoral dissertations *and* I'm also a published and award-winning poet and novelist. That artist/education/ professor background has led me to some experiences and conclusions about the creative process that may be a little different from those you usually read about in books like this, and which have in turn led me to writing this book.[1]

In 1977, I was working on my first book-length scholarly tome, my dissertation, and the placement office called up and asked me whether I wanted a part-time job in the education of the gifted. I jumped at the chance to make some money, as my university doctoral fellowship had run out. For my interview, I went to the library and read up about gifted children. During the preparation for the interview, I looked at the federal categories of giftedness. These were (1) superior cognitive ability, (2) specific academic ability, (3) visual and performing arts ability, (4) psychomotor ability, and (5) *creative thinking ability.*

Now this experience is where the dissonance that precipitated this book began.

How are people "gifted" in "creative thinking," I asked myself? I understood about very smart people, people who were better at one school subject than another, people who were gifted at visual arts, theater, music, and dance, and people who were good at various individual sports, but creative thinking? I asked myself, "Aren't smart people creative? Aren't people good at academic subjects creative? Aren't visual and performing artists creative? Aren't athletes creative? Why is there a separate category for creativity? Aren't all children creative, unless they've been abused or something?"

Hold that thought.

The Dissonance Between My Creative Life and My Paying Job

For extra money, while getting my Ph.D., I had applied and was accepted by the Ohio Arts Council to be a teaching artist as a Poet in the Schools in the National Endowment for the Arts "Artist in the Schools" program. My dual life as an artist and as an education scholar had begun, as I published my first creativity article, and my first article submitted to a scholarly journal, in the *Gifted Child Quarterly*, on incubation in the creative process, and later presented my first creativity study at a national conference, a survey of my fellow writers in the Artist in the Schools program about their lives and their creative processes. This was soon after I began my career in the education of the gifted and talented.

Over the next thirteen years I was a county program administrator and coordinator in Ohio and Michigan, and the principal of New York City's Hunter College Elementary School, the oldest U. S. school for gifted children. I published scholarly articles and conducted small studies, all the while being active in writing and submitting literary work as well. This dual life, as both an artist and a teacher of teachers has given me a different view of creativity than that of most of the people who are experts in the psychology of creativity. I had an earlier master's degree in English, and another in guidance and counseling, but I was making my living in the K-12 schools as an administrator.

The field of the education of the gifted and talented has one of its focuses on creativity, on teaching for creativity, and on researching creativity. There is a Creativity division in the National Association for Gifted Children organization, and the special interest group for the American Educational Research Association is named Research on the Gifted, Creative, and Talented. After I began working in rural Ohio as one of the first coordinators of programs for the gifted in Ohio, I got myself trained in many of the current (and still ongoing—not much has changed since the 1970s) creativity training programs – Creative Problem-Solving, Future Problem-Solving, Odyssey of the Mind, Lateral Thinking. I began to think about my own creative process. I learned firsthand from California's Mary Meeker about the Structure of the Intellect[2], and became one of her first advanced trainers, going around the country giving workshops on Guilford's theory of intellect, and on divergent production—fluency, flexibility, and elaboration, synthesis, and the like.[3]

Then I would go home and write my literary works, send them out for possible publication, and receive many rejections and enough acceptances to keep me going. My own creative life contained little of what I was learning about how to be creative in those workshops I attended, no matter how fun and how informative they were (and are)— little of brainstorming, SCAMPERing, generating of alternative solutions, creative thinking hats, or creative problem-solving, as described by the flow chart handouts I had been given.[4]

The creative process as described in educational and industrial psychology, was (and still is) fixed upon strategies I never used when I was doing my own creative work (nor did anyone else I knew—artists or educators). In fact, the creative process that business and education used was based on models that were designed for industry, and not for creators in other domains. Several companies have as their purpose to consult with industry to help business people be more creative. However, these strategies gained wide acceptance and practice in the educational world.

One technique widely taught is the Creative Problem Solving process, which is workshopped, taught, and researched at the Creative Education Foundation, which was founded in the early 1950s by advertising manager Alex Osborn, who published his famous book, *Applied Imagination*, in 1953, and who was a co-founder of the Institute after the book became a best-seller and he was able to leave advertising to focus on creativity education.[5] The Institute has conducted research on creativity testing and has published books by well-known educators and thinkers in creativity, giftedness, and spirituality. Their workshops are widely attended and they teach creativity at schools all over the world. Thus. a model intended for business was intentionally and successfully modified for schools.

I believe one cannot teach people to be creative without having experienced the creative process in a transformational way. What I'm going to teach you in this book, I've taught to many adults, mostly educators, in several states and on several continents. I believe teachers who say "I am not creative," who haven't even tried to be creative, who are reluctant and shy about their own creative personalities, selves, and practices, will not be able to help their students to be creative.

If you'll take a look at the extensive reference list and the endnotes for this book, you'll see that I have given detailed examples about their creative processes from the lives of real creators in science, mathematics, invention, business, visual arts, creative writing, music, theater, and physical performance (dance and athletics). These are creators who have enough eminence to have biographical works, interviews, or articles about them and their lives. What I will talk about in this book, what I am teaching you here, is supported by biographical data, examples, anecdotes, and memories told by the creators themselves or recorded by their biographers. In other words, these strategies are research-based. I have varied the examples by domain, to make a comprehensive picture of the creative process.

Chapter One is a chapter on how creativity fits into education and psychology, and how the creative process requires a certain type of personality, motivation, and passion. This is the requisite theory chapter, often the most boring chapter in a book, but always necessary, to lay the groundwork for what ensues.

Chapter Two presents the Five Core Attitudes for Creativity. My organizational strategy is to present an overview of the concept, and examples of how creators practiced the concept. Then I give an example (or several) that one could use for teaching about it to a class or group, perhaps for staff development. Then I give an example of how an individual could practice this concept; then there are a series of suggestions for how teachers can embed the concept into the classroom curriculum, in atmosphere, setting, or subject matter. Each section ends with a blank page for you, the reader, to add your own ideas for using the concept being discussed. My purpose is not to exhaustively give example after example, but to point the teacher/reader in the direction of **application** of the concept.

Chapter Three talks about many kinds of inspiration. Inspiration is one of the Seven I's for Creativity. Chapter Four continues, with the other six I's for creativity, Intuition, Improvisation, Imagination, Imagery, Incubation, and Insight. Chapter Five demonstrates certain general practices for the creative process. Chapter Six talks about how to act creatively within an institution with an emphasis on situational factors that are necessary for creativity.

Each of the Five Core Attitudes, Seven I's, and General Practices for the Creative Process have suggestions for an individual, for a group, and ways teachers can emphasize them in their classrooms. For each there is a table of ways to embed the attitude, "I," or general practice. Many of these have been ideas shared in discussion and written down by real teachers who have been in a creativity group. These teachers were from all grades, pre-school through high school, and so the ideas vary, but they will give you a starting point for implementing these principles. The suggestions are organic and can be interwoven into the whole fabric of the classroom. Creative teachers may often use some or all of these strategies, There is no mystery to teaching creativity for 21st Century Skills, nor should you be afraid. You are already creative and so are your students.

Jane Piirto, 2011

ACKNOWLEDGEMENTS

The cover of this book was painted by Grant Gilsdorf. It is called *Tree of Life*. The painting is owned by me, with permission to use it as a cover from the artist. Gilsdorf is an art teacher in the Olentangy, Ohio Liberty High School and is a former student of mine. I acknowledge its visual power here.

The Piirto Pyramid of Talent Development was re-designed by Mike Ruhe of the Ashland University graphic design office. Thank you.

This book was begun while I was on Senior Faculty Study Leave, and I acknowledge the faculty development program at Ashland University, and the committee who chose the applicants. Thank you, Ashland University.

I worked on the earliest draft in the snowy winter in my home town, Ishpeming, Michigan, while watching the downy woodpeckers on the suet feeder outside the window next to my desk, in the home of my aged mother, whose companion I was during this time. Thank you, Mother. Your lifelong creativity is a constant inspiration to me.

I sent an early draft to my former student and now colleague and friend, teacher and singer songwriter Jennifer Allen, who encouraged me and who read with care and connection. She even printed it out at a copy shop so she could page through it. Thank you, Jennifer. Your encouragement kept me going. Thank you to other adjunct professors, co-authors, and co-presenters on creativity-related topics: teacher, author and Creative Anachronist George Johnson, and teacher, singer songwriter, poet, and artist F. Christopher Reynolds.

To Diane Montgomery, fellow Suomalainen tÿtÿ and soul sister in creativity studies. To Karen Rogers, for reading and commenting on a very early draft. To Michael Piechowski, who read and commented on a late draft. To Joel McIntosh whose Prufrock Press publishes my book, *Talented Children and Adults*. To Jim Webb and Jan Gore, of Great Potential Press, which publishes my book *Understanding Creativity*. To Barbara Bernstein at Hampton Press, which publishes my book, *"My Teeming Brain": Understanding Creative* Writers. To Judith Kerman at Mayapple Press, which keeps my book of poetry, *Saunas*, in print. To my co-author of a book on creativity in Finnish, *Luovuus*, (which I am unable to read) Kari Üusikylä, who reads my poem, "Grandma You Used To" in Finnish in his talks at various festivals. To my co-presenter on intuition, William Keilty. In memoriam, to Robert Fox and Mike Karni, publishers of my novel (*The Three-Week Trance Diet*, Carpenter Press) and my collected works (*A Location in the Upper Peninsula*, Sampo Publishing), whose estates gave me back the copyrights.

To editors Donald Ambrose, John Baer, Ronald Beghetto, Patty Burke, Bonnie Cramond, Tracy Cross, Anne Fishkin, Marvin Gold, Elena Gregorenko, Kim Haines, Norma Lu Halfenstein, Carole Ruth Harris, Ray Horn, Sandra Kay, James Kaufman, Scott Kaufman, Barbara Kerr, the late Joe Kincheloe, Carl Leggo, Elisa Mambrino, Bronwyn Macfarlane, Paula Olszewski-Kubilius, Steven Pfeiffer, David Preiss, Monica Prendergrast, Steven Pritzker, Mark Runco, Pauline Sashemina, Patrick

Slattery, Kirsi Tirri, Tamra Stambaugh, and Joyce VanTassel-Baska, for asking me to publish creativity-related chapters and articles in their edited books and encyclopedias.

Thanks to these 21st Century teachers/graduate students who gave me feedback on these ideas: Peggy Abell, Kathleen Adams, Patty Albert, Dana Albrecht, Melody Allen, Deborah Julia Almaguer, Karen Altzner, Kathy Anclien, Matthew Anderson, Kevin Andress, Joseph Armpriester, Joseph Armstrong, Linille Artwell, Jo Aspin, Jo Ellen, Sheila Austin, Amy Bain, Christina Balderaz, Paula Ball, Paula Elizabeth, Brenda Bandy, Janice Bartels, Laurie Batdorf, Sharon Bates, Jeanine Baxter, Linda Bayles, Kathleen Beatty, Anthony Beery, Sara Beichler, Claudia Beljin, Dixie Beltz, Kerri Benson, Emily Bice, Andrea Bigam, Penny Bing, Jeffrey Bitler, Melody Blake, Karen Blaker, Deborah Bodley, Mark Bohland, Debra Bolyard, Jessica Bowman, Nancy Boyer, Mary Bradburn, Karen Brandt, Tim Bray, Adelyn Brent, Tobi Briggs, Amanda Brinkman, Terri Bristor, Cheryl Brockman, James Browder, Sara Brown, Jon Brush, Sharman Buckalew, Karen Burkett, Wein Bush, Monica Butcher, Steve Butler, Jennifer Butt, Heather Cachat, Jennifer Call, Lynea Cameron, Elizabeth Campbell Laurie Campitelli, Faye Caner, Linda Carmichael, Mary Ellen Carras, Monica Carroll, Dale Casper, Denise Castner, Rebekah Catalfina, Judith Catozza, Kathleen Cermak, Sandra Christian, Julie Christianer, Kathryn Clarisey, Dianne Clay, Bob Cline, Anita Coen, Jul'Yanna Collier, Linda Commerford, Kristin Contini, Gretchen Cooper, Suzanne Cooper, Marti Cordray-Corno, Stephanie Corradini, Stephanie Cousino, Donovan Cox, Darlene Cribbs, Mary Crumm, Karin Daley, Deborah Daniel, Gina Daniels, Karen Davis, Hilarie Day, Karla DeMali, Natalie Dechant, Rebecca Delair, Donna Dieterich, Jeffrey Dilyard, Cheryl Dixon, Amy Doake, James Dockery, Lisa Dees, Margie Dresser-Vogel, Dionne Dukes, Jennifer Ebersole, Angela Edwards Lisa Edwards Anne Efremoff, Rebecca Elkevizth, Rebecca Fairbairn, Thomas Fairbanks, Chris Falkenberg, Julie Faller, Kristene Fauser, Krista Ferini, Aimee Fletcher, Christine Finney, Julia Frahm, Holly Fox, Kimberly Frasher, Joyce Fredricks, Heather Frost-Hauck, Brian Gale, Michelle Gdovin, Grant Gilsdorf, Jeanna Giovanelli, Jeanne Girbert, Lizbeth Gladwell, Maureen Gotterbarm, Dianne Griffin, Tracey Grimes, Rosanna Grooms, Chrisann Gross, Cynthia Grove, Terri Guertin, Stefanie Hall, Sonya Haller, Megan Hanchette, Michelle Haramia, Julia Hare, Cary Harrod, Charlene Hartley, Donna Hasel, Debra Hauer, Stacy Jo Hawthorne, Kellie Hayden, Colleen Haynes, Carol Heckaman, Mary Kay Helba, Jo Ann Henderson, Maryjo Hepler, Jaimee Herron, Aimee Hilsher, Julie Hinkle, Susan Hite, Sally Hose, Rebekah Hogue, Gina Hohman, Jessica Holland, Mary Hopkins, Suzanne Horner, Elizabeth Horton, Janice Hubbard, Jennifer Hummel, Laura Hunt, Tamara Jacobs, Deborah Jados, Janet Hames, Pamela James, Kely Janofa, Rebecca Johnson, Nicole Johnson, Jeanne Johnson, Traci Joynston, Charlotte Jones, Judith Jones, Karen Jones, Victoria Jones, Jennifer Kazmierczak, Anthony Keefer, Carole Keil, Rebecca Kendrick, Beth Kennedy, Rebecca Kendrick, Beth Kennedy, Beverly Kenney, Kent Kerns, Erin King, Sheryl King, Lynne Knapp, Jill Knapp, Lynnea Knobel, Joyce Knotts, Janice Kollar, Kim Koos, Rhonda Kostal, Lisa Lang, Jo Larson-Kish, Jacob Lees, Nicole Leimweber, Margaret Leutzinger, Raymond Lewis, Monica Lewis, Brady Liming, Ann Linn, Mary Beth

Liossis, Lin-Hsien Liu, Mary Lobuglio, Jennifer Looks, Amy Lott, Elizabeth MacDowell, Nora MacFarlane, Heidi MacNeal, Lindsay Mangas, Marianne Manley, Aimee Marburger, Wendy Marett, Sara Marino, Starrlet Martin, Gail Martino, Monica Mason, Monica Mason, Heather Massaro, Karen McDonough, Tanya McGregor Shayla McGuire, Alicia McKee, Esther McKenzie, Kathleen McPeek, Catherine Mellinger, Mary Jeanne Melvin, Michelle Merton, Dawn Metzger, Linda Michael, Joanne Miller, Jeri Millhouse, Sheri Mitchell, Jennifer Moody Ann Moody, Elizabeth Moore, Cynthia Moore, Jamie Morris, Vaughn Musser, Laura Nabors, Cynthia Nader, Andrew Naelitz, Susan Nash, JoAnne Neely, Varlorie Newman, Sandra Nicholson, Jessica Niekamp, Patricia Niewierski, Terri Noe, Megan Nolan, Denise Novak, Amy Novar, Patricia Nyquist Carol Oberholtzer, Gina Ogden, Jennifer Ohm, Melany Ondrus, Judith Oprandi, Kristi Ovak, Patricia Palko, Patricia Passwaters, Julie Paterson, Lea Paulsen, Lori Pavlik, Jane Payne, Cybele Pelka, Jennifer Pennell, Sue Pfister, Patricia Piron, Janice Prusha, Jodene Quinn, Donna Rains, Elizabeth Ray Beth Ray Lawrence Reams, Taita Reeder, Richard Reischman, Leslie Ressa, Martha Reyer, Janell Reynolds, Tina Rhine, Kay Rhyman, Rebekah Rice, Michelle Rice, Carolyn Richardson, Melissa Rimer, Cheryl Roberts, Mary Alice Robinson, Cynthia Rode, Victoria Roesch, Amy Rogers, Robbin Rogers, Sarah Rokoff, Shannen Rook, Leanne Ross, Amy Runser, Kristine Rutledge, Linda Salom, Elisa Schaffer, Pamela Schmuck, Katherine Schneider, Jennifer Sherman, Nicole Sherman, Tracy Shuld, Laruie Schultz, Gretchen Schuster, Cynthia Schutter, Amy Scott, Ruth Scott, Amy Scragg, Michelle Seitz, Melinda Semerar, Monica Shadle, Summer Shaffer, Monica Shaner, Donna Shaw, Nicole Sherman Alice Shoemaker, Susan Shultzman, Susan Simon, Eileen Sirgo, Terry Skudlarek, Kelly Smith, Colette Smith, Laura Kay Smith, Cynthia Smith, Connie Snyder, Goldie Spencer, Susan Stanfield, Tammy Starkey, Sandra Stephens, Laurie Stephenson, Caroline Stieg, Suzanne Ston, Thomas Strous, Cam Struck, Michelle Sundberg, Dianne Swain, Saundra Sweeney, Misty Swanger, Amy Tate, Holly Tetlow, Cam Thompson, Paul Thompson, Cynthia Tisue, Theresa Toadvine, Brenda Toler, Jackie Traini, John Trimner, Ellen Tucker, Kathrine Turner, Angela Ulrich, Jan Urankar, Lauren Valz, Dhana Vercruysse, Michelle Vrooman-Kennett, Bonnie Wachter, Kathryn Wagner, Lynn Wagner, Jane Warner, Amanda Warren, Peggy Sue Webb, Andrea Webb, Jessica Welker, Sharon Weller, Karen Westfall, Heidi Wheeler, Carissa Wiedle, Rhonda Williams, Jennifer Williams, Katrice Wright, Laura Wood, Laurie Anne Wood, Tracy Woodbury, Susan Woodmansee, Virgina Woodring, Jennifer Woods, Katrice Wright, Ashley Yontz, Lindsey Young, Meredith Young, Eileen Zech, Melinda Zellner, Kelli Zubovich.

AUTHOR BIOGRAPHY

Jane Piirto is Trustees' Distinguished Professor at Ashland University in Ohio. She is an award-winning scholar in education and psychology, and a widely published and award-winning poet and novelist. Her doctorate is in educational leadership. She has worked with students pre-K to doctoral level as a teacher, administrator, and professor.

Her scholarly books are *Talented Children and Adults* (3 editions), *Understanding Those Who Create* (2 editions, 2nd edition Parents' Choice & Glyph Awards); *Understanding Creativity*; *Luovuus*; and *"My Teeming Brain": Understanding Creative Writers*. She has published many scholarly articles in peer-reviewed journals and anthologies.

Her literary books are *The Three-Week Trance Diet* (award-winning novel); *A Location in the Upper Peninsula* (collected poems, stories, essays) and *Saunas* (poems), as well as several poetry and creative nonfiction chapbooks. She has won Individual Artist Fellowships from the Ohio Arts Council in both poetry and fiction.

She is listed as both a poet and a writer in the Directory of American Poets and Writers.

She is a recipient of the Mensa Lifetime Achievement Award by the Mensa Education and Research Foundation, and of an honorary Doctor of Humane Letters degree by her undergraduate alma mater, Northern Michigan University. She was named an *Ohio Magazine* educator of distinction, and was awarded the Higher Education Award from the Ohio Association for Gifted Children. In 2010 she was named Distinguished Scholar by the National Association for Gifted Children.

She has given over 1,000 speeches, consultations, and workshops.

CREATIVITY FOR 21ST CENTURY SKILLS

Personality, Motivation, Study, and Talent

Currently, there is a call for 21st Century Skills, and these skills include creativity skills. This book will, perhaps help in that endeavor.

These 21st Century Skills include creativity and innovation skills within a comprehensive skills framework, as suggested by one of the 21st Century Skills think tanks. These are operationally defined, as follows.[6]

Think Creatively

1. Use a wide range of idea creation techniques (such as brainstorming)
2. Create new and worthwhile ideas (both incremental and radical concepts)
3. Elaborate, refine, analyze and evaluate their own ideas in order to improve and maximize creative efforts

Work Creatively with Others

4. Develop, implement and communicate new ideas to others effectively
5. Be open and responsive to new and diverse perspectives; incorporate group input and feedback into the work
6. Demonstrate originality and inventiveness in work and understand the real world limits to adopting new ideas
7. View failure as an opportunity to learn; understand that creativity and innovation is a long-term, cyclical process of small successes and frequent mistakes

Implement Innovations

8. Act on creative ideas to make a tangible and useful contribution to the field in which the innovation will occur

When people speak or think of creativity, they mistakenly think of it as having only to do with the visual arts and the other arts. Creativity cuts across all areas, and has to do with making new in all domains.

A few of the skills called for above (1, 3) focus on divergent thinking, a concept (that is over 60 years old), sometimes confused with creativity. Other skills (2, 4, 5, 6, 7, 8) focus on what I am going to write about in this book. Creativity is simply defined here, as "to make something new," as a prerequisite to innovation.

Divergent thinking was part of the psychologist J. P. Guilford's Structure of Intellect. In 1950, Guilford, who was then President of the American Psychological Association, gave a speech that is often called the beginning of the modern interest in creativity as a measurable phenomenon. Guilford theorized that there are 120 kinds of measurable intelligence factored across five operations, four contents, and six products. One of the five operations was *divergent thinking*. His attempt to create a measurable phenomenon still challenges researchers, who often fail at defining creativity and thus fail to measure it.

J. P. Guilford differentiated between "convergent" thinking and "divergent" thinking. Convergent thinking emphasizes remembering what is known, being able to learn what exists, and being able to save that information in one's brain, being able to find the correct answer—i.e., converge. Divergent thinking emphasizes the revision of what is already known, of exploring what can be known, and of building new information—i.e. diverge. People who prefer the convergent mode of intellect supposedly tend to do what is expected of them, while those who prefer the divergent mode of intellect supposedly tend to take risks and to speculate.

Divergent production has often been confused with creativity. Here are Guilford's original factors that make up divergent production: "sensitivity to problems, ideational fluency, flexibility of set, ideational novelty, synthesizing ability, analyzing ability, reorganizing or redefining ability, span of ideational structure, and evaluating ability."[7] He developed tests to measure each of these. Whole industries of exercise books, curricula, assessment systems, and suggestions have been based on the psychometrically measured Guilfordian "operation" of divergent production. I will include a short discussion and an exercise in divergent production in Chapter 4.

Creativity has been a topic of discussion and of research in the field of psychology for approximately sixty years. Psychology is the parent discipline of education, and education often takes its definitions from psychology. Psychology, the scientific study of mental operations and behavior, asks: What makes people creative? How can creativity be measured? How can creativity be enhanced? What can we learn from creative adults that will help us raise more creative children? Is creativity an aptitude? Is creativity ability? Is creativity a domain? Is creativity acquired? Is creativity innate? What happens in the mind while a person is creating? What are the conditions for creative production? What inhibits creative production? What does the social setting contribute to creativity? Is creativity a solitary or community activity? All these, and more, are questions psychologists have sought to study with regard to creativity. Creativity research usually follows four streams, called the "4 P's": Process, Product, Person, and Press (meaning environmental influence).

Educators nowadays are focusing on a set of recommendations called 21st century skills, and among these are creativity skills. Perhaps it's time to join the 21st century, and to add to the divergent production exercises that flood the creativity enhancement market in education, and move into a new set of skills that take into account the *whole* person, the *whole* teacher, the "interior teacher," as popular educator Parker Palmer called it.[8] This book will add to the literature on the interior lives of teachers, with an emphasis on new sets of skills. See Table 1.1.

Table 1.1. How 21st century skills and Piirto's creativity system relate

21ST CENTURY CREATIVITY SKILLS	PIIRTO'S CREATIVITY SYSTEM
Think Creatively	
1. Use a wide range of idea creation techniques (such as brainstorming)	– Core Attitudes (Openness to Experience, Risk-Taking, Tolerance for AmbiguityI's (Inspiration, Intuition Insight, Imagination, Imagery, Incubation,) – General Aspects (Exercise)
2. Create new and worthwhile ideas (both incremental and radical concepts)	– Core Attitudes (Openness to Experience, Risk-Taking, Tolerance for Ambiguity, Self-Discipline, Group Trust) – Seven I's – General Aspects
3. Elaborate, refine, analyze and evaluate their own ideas in order to improve and maximize creative efforts	– Core Attitudes (Openness to Experience, Risk-Taking, Tolerance for Ambiguity. – I's (Incubation, Intuition) – General Aspects
Work Creatively with Others	
4. Develop, implement and communicate new ideas to others effectively	– Core Attitudes (Openness to Experience, Risk-Taking, Tolerance for Ambiguity, Group Trust) – I's (Imagination, Imagery, Improvisation, General Aspects
5. Be open and responsive to new and diverse perspectives; incorporate group input and feedback into the work	– Core Attitudes (Group Trust)
6. Demonstrate originality and inventiveness in work and understand the real world limits to adopting new ideas	– Core Attitudes (Tolerance for Ambiguity; Self-Discipline; Group Trust) – I's (Intuition Inspiration, Incubation) – General Aspects (Creativity as the Process of a Life)
7. View failure as an opportunity to learn; understand that creativity and innovation is a long-term, cyclical process of small successes and frequent mistakes	– Core Attitudes (Openness to Experience, Risk-Taking, Tolerance for Ambiguity, Self-Discipline) – General Aspects (Creativity as the Process of a Life)
Implement Innovations	
8. Act on creative ideas to make a tangible and useful contribution to the field in which the innovation will occur	– Core Attitudes (Tolerance for Ambiguity Self-Discipline; Group Trust) – I's (Intuition Inspiration Incubation) – General Practices (Creativity as the Process of a Life)

Successful creators in domains have similar patterns of education and familial influence, depending on the *domain* in which the creativity is practiced.[9] I have studied persons by domain of creativity rather than by general creativity aptitude, with a view to how their life paths can inform the creative process.[10] That is, most of my research has been on the Person and Press, with very little emphasis on the Product. Each domain has its own rules of accomplishment and paths to achievement. However, as I was reading biographies, interviews, and memoirs and plotting life paths and thinking about the environmental suns, as delineated in my model, The Piirto Pyramid (see Appendix), I inevitably came upon the creative process as practiced by creators. I noticed that no matter what a creator creates, the creative process is remarkably similar. There are commonalities across domains.

Most creative adults in the domains of visual arts, literature, science, mathematics, music, acting, athletics, invention, entrepreneurship, and dance talked about their creative process in what could be called holistic, or organic terms, rather than in step-by-step linear progressions.[11]

Cognitive psychologists disparage such accounts, which they call anecdotal and retrospective, and therefore untrustworthy, saying that you can't trust what people say about their own creative processes, because how can they know what's really happening inside.[12] Such disparaging of the biographical is a common practice for scientifically oriented psychologists who distrust any findings that are not made with double-blind experiments. But my literary background, which dwelt on the *poetic way of knowing* that embraces the psychoanalytic and the depth psychological viewpoints of Freud, Jung, and Hillman,[13] caused me to doubt the psychologically scientific and to search for the experiential, the affective, and the artistic in these biographical descriptions.

As I studied the creative processes of creators, I found no mention of the words creative problem-solving, fluency, flexibility, brainstorming, or elaboration in the essays, memoirs, biographies, and interviews of creators in various domains. The creative process as practiced by creative productive adults has engaged thinkers of the world from prehistoric times, but none of them has described the creative process in the way that it has been taught in schools for the past fifty years. For example, mythological and classical perspectives on the creative process have viewed inspiration as the visitation of the Muse,[14] which is the inspiration of desire, or of love, but a discussion of love is often confused with a discussion of sex, and the schools step back from such discussions.

Historically, the creative process has also been tied with desire for spiritual unity, and when people describe their creative process, they often get dreamy and intense. Schools focus on the concrete, and any venture into the mystical or spiritual is often confused with the teaching of religion, which is banned in public schools. The creative process is also tied with the desire for personal expression. People who create also express their autobiographical experiences, their coded stories, their past traumas, their obsessions, and their passions. While the personal is often evoked in school in the form of journals or essays, the most value is placed on the expository, the impersonal, and the evaluative.

The concept of two sides of the brain, the right side for creativity and the left side for plodding intellect, is part of overly simplistic contemporary understanding of creativity. (Indeed, we need the whole brain for creative production.)[15] What is popularly called "right-brain thinking," is often considered flakey and not trustworthy, and, therefore, "creative," in quotation marks, is often a put-down.

Those who are creative seem to follow certain common practices. Even the most recent biographical accounts describe experiences similar to those of yore. Creators in the sixteenth century accessed practices remarkably similar to creators in the twenty-first century, yet these practices are glossed over in the creativity books that fill the book stalls at exhibit halls at education conferences. In the domain of education, we rely upon psychology to lead us, and the psychologists, especially the educational psychologists, seem to be still in Guilford's cognitive (mind) view. Remember, he called his theory the Structure of the *Intellect*. Another multi-factored theorist in psychology, Howard Gardner, has called his eight types of intelligences, frames of *mind*, and each of his books has the word "mind" in the title. The body and the heart are minimized in these theories (though two of Gardner's intelligences are the interpersonal and the kinesthetic).

The repertoires of many of those who teach people to be creative, who often use only strategies based on Guilford's cognitive aspect of divergent production in enhancing creativity, should be expanded.

Many of the creative and productive adults whose lives are worthy of scholarly biographies seemed to have creative processes that could be divided into three themes, with several subthemes. (1) They seemed to have certain core attitudes toward creativity; (2) they experienced what I came to call the Seven I's (Inspiration, Insight, Intuition, Incubation, Improvisation, Imagery, Imagination) (3) they engaged in *certain* general practices: a need for solitude and for rituals; they had formally studied their domains; they liked meditative practices; they were part of a community of people working in the same domain; their creativity was part of a lifestyle, a lifelong process.

I have collapsed these into what I call the *Five Core Attitudes for Creativity, the Seven I's for Creativity*, and the *General Practices for Creativity*, and I began to translate these concepts into lessons. Not all creators use all of these techniques, but many creators use at least some of the techniques. Why can't people who want to be more creative, and people who teach people to be more creative, try to duplicate, or imitate what the creative producers of works of art, science, invention, and music, say they do while they create?

By now, I have assembled many activities that tap into the mysterious, nebulous, dreamy, solitary, quietness of the creative process as it has been written about and talked about by adult creators. I have asked my teacher students in creativity classes to try these activities, and to translate the principles upon which the activities are based, into activities that would be able to be used by the children and adolescents they teach.[16]

Over the years, a thousand or so of my undergraduate and graduate students have completed biographical studies that illuminate the themes in creators' lives, and how they create. Students are to analyze the life path and creative process of the creator according to the theoretical framework of my Pyramid of Talent Development. (See Appendix A for an explanation of the Piirto Pyramid of Talent Development.) Results show that the patterns in creative lives that I have delineated in my two books, *Talented Children and Adults*, and *Understanding Creativity*, seem to hold up.

I have presented these ideas about the creative process in real creators to thousands of people at psychology and education conferences and at workshops. While my work has been with teachers and college students, and not with business people, the other great consumers of materials on creativity, perhaps what is here described can be extrapolated.

The Thorn Of Creativity Is Necessary

On my Pyramid of Talent Development there is a thorn. The thorn compels the person to create. Often, the creative person decides to pursue the development of his or her creative talent after some catalyst reveals that this is what must happen. It may be winning a contest or receiving praise or becoming so pleasantly engrossed in the making that is creating that the person realizes that this is what he or she must do come hell or high water. It may be a depression that is assuaged by making or creating, so much so that the self-healing that happens when one is creative warns the person that he or she must create in order to prevent illness. It may come after a long period of thought and meditation. The creative person recognizes that the thorn is pricking and the call must be answered. Here is a drawing one of my group members made to illustrate a quotation about the thorn of creative passion; one cannot not do what it pricks at.

Jung described the creative person, the "poet" (by this he was Platonic and Aristotelian, using the term "poet" to indicate all those who create) and his or her "art" (by this he meant *poesis*, the work the creative person does) thus: "Art is a kind of innate drive that seizes a human being and makes him its instrument. The artist is not a person endowed with free will who seeks his own ends, but one

Figure 1. "They Can't Not Write".

who allows art to realize its purpose through him."[17] Jung commented that the lives of such creators are often unsatisfactory on the personal level because "a person must pay dearly for the divine gift of the creative fire."

Carl Jung believed that people are bestowed with certain talents when they are born–he called this "energy." Because this energy is so all-powerful, creators may exhibit "ruthlessness, selfishness, and vanity" (he commented on the narcissistic personalities of creators), but this could be excused because of the calling, which, from birth, pursues the creator to interpret the world by being subordinate to his talent.

The poet (creator) gives his or her talent form in the domain in which he or she works. Thus the "great work of art is like a dream" that "does not explain itself and is never unequivocal."[18] The dream portrays an image, and this image is reflective of what Jungians call the objective psyche or collective unconscious, something bigger than the person him- or herself, a representation, an interpretation, of what exists in the spiritual nature of the society. The life of the creator does not explain the work, interesting though the life may be. The work itself is its own explanation.

So, let us consider then our paradoxical image of a thorn. Immediately we picture the thorn on a stem. The stem is essential to the thorn, for the thorn cannot exist without the nourishment from the stem rooted in the earth, within the eco-system, the planet, the cosmos. Raising our focus upward, we see the thorn protects the stem, upon which grows the rose. All are part of the image of the thorn. The rose is contained in the thorn and the thorn protects the rose. The rose is the symbol, or the image, of multitudinous meanings, many sentimental, many intertwined with religion, royalty, and mystery. Whatever the image is, the rose can become–the thorn, which can prick, stab, or loosen the flesh which tries to capture it, to hold it, protects it. Conversely, where lives are loosened and pierced, be it traumatic, ecstatic, or both, the thorn calls attention to a deeply rooted unfolding, blossoming, always more.

Musician Quincy Jones is an example. At age eleven, he broke into a warehouse and found a piano. "I touched that piano and every cell in my body said this is what you will do for the rest of your life," he said. He would revisit that piano to learn songs he'd heard his neighbor Lucy play. He began composing music before he knew what a key signature was. When he heard a local barber playing the trumpet, he was hooked on playing it also, but he tried everything from violin to the sousaphone before he finally got his hands on a trumpet.[19] He said, "that when he got a trumpet, "the love, this passion came forth, and that's when somebody lit a flame, a candle inside, and that candle still burns, you know, it never went out. I'd stay up all night sometimes until my eyes bled to write the music."

MOTIVATION TO CREATE: PASSION FOR WORK IN A DOMAIN

Motivation to create has to do with The Thorn. The main cause for creativity is that the creative person *wants* to be creative, in whatever domain he or she is working – whether it be woodworking in the basement, dancing, acting, drawing, singing, doing science, mathematics, inventing, being an entrepreneur, being an athlete, cooking, sewing, building, designing. People who are creative must have motivation.[20] Creators *intend* to be creative, to make—something. People have to *want* to be creative. Creativity takes a long time and a certain amount of obsession. Motivation is the only and main personality attribute that all creative people have and need.[21] The creator prepares by study and mental readiness. Creative people want and need to make things in their domains of interest. They also possess the talent necessary to create in their domains, and they have had the environmental influence necessary. These environmental influences include beginning family influences.

We can extrapolate from psychological work on reward. What are the rewards for being creative? Fame is not usually one of them. Musician Mat Callahan said, "I have never found any correlation between money and the effectiveness of the creative process and its results." He went on: "Do I produce a demand for my creative work ... do I produce marketable commodities? Maybe. Do I apply my energies to my creative work, regardless? Certainly. Continuously. Why? Because of the satisfaction I derive from the process itself and the pleasure it brings to others."[22]

The most enriching rewards for creative endeavor are intrinsic; that is, the reward is in the pleasure the creator takes in doing the work itself, and in achieving the result, and not from the pay or the prize. Even painters who don't have galleries, musicians who don't have audiences, writers who aren't published, actors who act in community theater, dancers who dance alone, scientists and mathematicians who spread the table with arcane formulas to solve personally challenging problems, do not stop doing. While some may say that creative people need a killer instinct, and need to be so driven that they would do anything for fame, recognition, or validation, continued creative production derives from less cruel motives. The work itself is intrinsically interesting.

Often, the thorn, the passion that wounds, also saves. The obsession that is ingrained in the image can serve to rescue someone who is lost. Musician Eric Clapton suffered from heroin addiction and from alcoholism. His girlfriend indulged in drugs and alcohol with him. After two stints in rehab, Clapton was able to quit, and has remained sober for over twenty years. He said that it was his desire to play and create music that saved him. His girlfriend was not so fortunate, for she had no passion for creating. She died after many relapses, saying that she had nothing else but the addiction, and that she was unable to give it up.[23]

Thus, the creative process is not merely as described or practiced by the educational and psychology experts. It is more complex. Often the creative process is similar to a spiritual or a transformational practice in creators. Some have said that God draws people to himself through creativity.[24] Creators are often apt to closely guard the mysteries of the creative process, and to treat the creative process ritualistically.

Personal transformation is often necessary so the person who wants to create will slough off the reasons not to create. You can't teach students to be creative unless you have tried out your own creative impulses. And everyone is creative, and has creative impulses. Often, placing yourself into proximity to other creators, and practicing a process whether or not you believe it will work, is enough to make it work. Lassitude, laziness, inertia—all operate in preventing us from creating.

Rejection, indifference, and criticism from others also thwart creativity. Fear of creating also has a place in obstructing the creative process. Many of my students are female teachers who have such busy lives as mothers, wives, and professionals, that they have forgotten who they are, essentially, who they were before they led lives of sacrifice for love, and they often experience a deep feeling of coming home during the creativity class.

DO YOU HAVE THE PERSONALITY TO BE CREATIVE?

Certain personality characteristics are common in creators, as you can see on the base of the Piirto Pyramid.[25]

Which of these do you have? Look at the following list. Think about a time in your life when you showed this personality characteristic and tell a story about that time. This may take some time, but it may be fun for you to recall your own past personality-driven experiences and acts. In a class, perhaps a few minutes at the beginning or during each or several class periods can be given to doing this.

Table 1.2. My personality attributes

MY PERSONALITY ATTRIBUTES	MY STORY: WHEN I SHOWED THIS ATTRIBUTE
Androgyny—a balance of masculinity and femininity	
Imagination	
Introversion	
Intuition	
Independence	
Naiveté, Or Openness To Experience,	
Conscientiousness	
Creativity	
Perceptiveness	
Persistence	
Preference For Complexity	
Resilience	
Risk-taking	
Self-discipline	
Perfectionism (self)	
Tolerance For Ambiguity	
Motivation to Create	
Intensity (overexcitability in intellect, emotion, imagination, sensation, or physicality[26]	

If you are curious about which personality attributes you prefer, take an online personality test or two. The one I most often work with is the Myers-Briggs Type Indicator, which was one of the tests developed when they began researching the personalities of creative adults in Berkeley, California in the early 1950s.[27] The Myers-Briggs Type Indicator also has a creativity scale. The research on the creative personality has gone on for over 50 years, and the early findings still hold true. As Frank Barron, one of the primary researchers said in 1968, "Three distinct traits characterize creative people: (a) they discern more complexity than others, (b) they possess more perceptual openness and resist premature judgmental closure, and they depend on intuition and hunches to a great degree. Finally, creative people seem motivated to create since they often expend a great amount of energy on their productions."[28]

If you don't think you show these personality characteristics, don't despair. None of this is set in stone. The major point here is that you have the thorn and you have the motivation.

DO YOU KNOW THE DOMAIN?

Besides the thorn and the motivation, you have to know what you're doing. This will entail study, if you want to get serious about the creativity. Knowledge of the domain in which a person wants to work is absolutely necessary. In teaching, people take classes in how to teach, and in classroom management. The people who observe a teacher managing a class don't even know he or she is managing, the class procedures are so seamless. This is knowing the domain. Pulitzer prize-winning composer John Adams said,

> There's no substitute for having plain, awesome musical chops: having a great ear, being able to perform well on an instrument, and having a huge, encyclopedic knowledge of music. Composers should know everything. Nowadays there's no excuse for not being at least aurally familiar with medieval music and Renaissance music, and they should know jazz and pop music, too. It's all possible to do.[29]

The formal study that is necessary to create within a domain cannot be short-circuited. Expertise is necessary. The rule of thumb is called The Ten Year Rule; that is, one should have studied a domain for about ten years before one can make an original contribution. They also say that you should do 10,000 repetitions.[30] This varies by domain of creativity, but the point is that if you are interested in doing something, you should study it, preferably in a formal way. You're not going to invent a new car design without studying car design and know what has been done before, what didn't work, what worked, and where the car design field can be pushed.

In studies I did of published and award-winning creative writers, I found that almost all of them majored in literature as undergraduates, before they turned to creative writing as a profession. They had read literature and studied it before they were accepted as writing it.[31]

Many people say, "I am not creative, never have been, never will be." Others say, "I wish I were more creative but don't know how to be." In my practice as a professor who teaches teachers, I have often heard both of these statements. Teachers are urged to teach their students to be creative, but the teachers themselves are often reluctant, fearful, and uneducated in how to do so. My belief is that the teachers must themselves be transformed in order to teach their students to be creative.

The following pages will, I hope, lead to your, the reader's own "aha!," and contribute to your own transformation into being a more creative person than you have been in the past. I will discuss each of the Five Core Attitudes, Seven I's, and General Practices, giving examples from the lives of eminent creators, and giving examples of exercises you can try either with a group or by yourself.

As a teacher I ask myself one question each time I plan a lesson. How can I help my students take the concept I am teaching about into their own physical reality? If we do not do it physically, with our senses, we are likely to not take it in completely. (That is the reason we remember our gym classes more than our math classes.) How can I as a teacher create a lesson that will make an image? How can I make the concept concrete? "What is the image?" is my teaching motto. Every time I am teaching something and every time I am writing something, I try to create the image or the experience so that my students and my listeners can create the image. So far it has seemed to work.

What is personal transformation, after all? Many writers on the topic use the image of the caterpillar transforming into a butterfly.[32] I think that is a little cliché and corny, but the image, being a standard science lesson for kindergartners, whose teachers show them chrysalises from which butterflies emerge, has the advantage that everyone will get it. Personal transformation means that a person will become more intensely and wholly who she is and has always potentially been. In the process, the person experiences a sense of recognition through the revelation provided by the images that have been created. The truth emerges and the person feels more wholly her ideal self. This is an inner process in which the person blooms forth in becoming what is possible. The person then, in turn, may sway others to experience their own creative transformations.

I am not a therapist, nor do I claim to have discovered the meaning of life, nor do I claim to be a healer or a leader to anyone but my students, and that always ends when the semester ends, and so I urge you to seek your own transformative images through some of the following practices.

SUMMARY OF KEY POINTS

1. The 21st Century Skills movement has stated that creativity is important.
2. Many of the creativity skills currently taught are based on a theory of divergent production that is over 60 years old.
3. New skills should be based on what real creators do while they create.
4. The guiding framework for this book comes from the author's model/image of a pyramid and suns.
5. Personality attributes, cognitive ability, talent, environmental factors, motivation, and knowledge of the field are necessary in developing one's creativity.
6. Creativity enhancement is often a transformative process for the individual.

MY THOUGHTS AND INSIGHTS ON THE IDEAS IN THIS CHAPTER

Possibilities:

– Fill out your own Pyramid of Talent Development, based on the figure in Appendix A.
– What is your "thorn"?
– Discuss your motivation for creating.
– Discuss your training, study, and development in a domain.
– Make an image (drawing, creative writing, music, photography, dance, diagram, etc.) of some idea in this chapter.

FIVE CORE ATTITUDES

This chapter will discuss the five core attitudes creative people seem to possess: (1) Core attitude of Self-discipline about doing the creative work, which includes the presence of motivation; (2) core attitude of Naiveté, or openness to experience; (3) core attitude of Risk-taking; (4) core attitude of Tolerance for Ambiguity; (5) core attitude of Group Trust.

One of the most common practices among all creators is the fact that they make notes to themselves of ideas that occur to them. The notes are written in personal code. In order to begin to practice the five core attitudes, buy a sketchbook from the local drugstore. It should be small enough to be mobile, to be put into a purse, pocket, or briefcase. Alternately, always make sure to have a stub of pencil and a scrap of paper, to make notes and marks. So. Begin. Take yourself and your ideas seriously. *Jot your thoughts*. The notes and marks are just that, messages to yourself, not to be interpreted by anyone else but you, the maker of the marks. I call this a Thoughtlog because the content is thoughts. No one else has to be able to understand it.

CORE ATTITUDE OF SELF-DISCIPLINE

When one studies the lives of creators, one often finds they have created many, many works, even though they may be only known for one, two, or a few. This production of multiples takes self-discipline, and the self-discipline leads to the great productivity of creators. Expertise research says that one cannot contribute anything new to a domain unless one has been working in the domain for at least ten years.[33] Expertise is acquired after one has done 10,000 or more repetitions, which is called *deliberate practice*. As a result of this exposure to the domain, an expert can recognize what's wrong instantaneously, and move to fix it. Experts in a domain have developed their long-term memories, and can retrieve information that is pertinent to the problem at hand, and immediately, or with some thought, figure out what needs to be done.

The expertise research downplays the existence of domain talent as well as creativity ability as too nebulous, too un-quantifiable, too abstract, and seeks to extrapolate how people acquire the skills to make what they will make. Expertise is acquired by focusing on certain skills polished by deliberate practice, and the question that is often asked is whether deliberate practice can account for differences between those who are considered "more talented" and those who are considered "less talented." The expertise people do not doubt that innate differences exist, but they are seeking to find out whether these differences account for the ultimate levels of accomplishment certain individuals can achieve.

The creator has acquired *automaticity*, the ability to do the task without thinking. Picture the piano student, practicing scales for hours, logging constant and continuous days and months in the practice room. Picture the athlete, doing drills for hours, logging constant and continuous days and months on the practice court.

Picture the writer, sitting alone at the desk, writing poems and stories and novels, with only a few published. Picture the teacher, glancing at student papers and immediately being able to figure out how it can be improved, and what needs to be done when the student revises. Picture the aged visual artist Willem de Kooning, who, even after he had achieved fame and notoriety, would spend hours drawing portraits of the people he saw on television. [34] All of these creators have acquired expertise.

Examples from Creators of the Core Attitude of Self-Discipline

Van Gogh wrote to his brother Theo, an art dealer, "I am daily working on drawing figures. I shall make a hundred of them before I paint them."[35] Visual artist Josef Albers said, "In science one plus one is two, but in art it can be three. Often I have to paint a picture ten different times before I reach a realization. I usually start with a small sketch, then comes painting after painting until I realize what I'm after."[36]

Choreographer Agnes de Mille noted that "all artists—indeed all great careerists—submit themselves, as well as their friends, to lifelong, relentless discipline, largely self-imposed and never for any reason relinquished."[37] Most well known creators are known for only a few of their voluminous numbers of creative works, produced through great self-discipline over a period of years.

Composer William Bolcom said, "For a big piece, I pull together a big morgue of sketches — little notations, jottings that will remind me of how a particular passage might go. When there are enough of these things, I'm ready to write. That's exactly what happened with the *Songs of Innocence* and of *Experience*. Suddenly I realized that I was ready to start, I was ready to get the thing done, after sketching, working on bits and pieces, for quite a number of years."[38]

Exercise for a Group or for Staff Development

In creativity group, group members use their Thoughtlogs to signify the importance of repetitive practice. The Thoughtlogs are solitary creative practice, as well as practice in the core attitude of self-discipline. The group members must make marks for 10 minutes a day. "Making marks" means anything—not only writing. Sometimes, literally, the page for the day has consisted of one pencil slash. These are not judged nor commented upon; e.g., this is not a dialogue between teacher and student as journals often are, but an attempt to imitate the creative practice of creators; who all make marks about their products; they do not hold them in their heads and produce them full-blown, as Venus rises from the sea.

To form a habit takes about 21 days to 2 months, according to popular internet sources. This requirement has had various results; one student used the sketches in her Thoughtlog for her senior art show; others have not continued the practice, but have looked back on the 15 weeks of creativity group and find there a portrait of their lives at that time. They did not take the "habit" of creative thinking to its regular deliberate practice, because they were not motivated to do so.

Exercise to Do Alone

Practice. You want to become an actor, a dancer, an athlete, a scientist, a mathematician, a musician, a creative writer, a visual artist? A teacher? Practice. One of the funniest examples (in a sad way) of a teacher acquiring expertise is in the movie *Chalk*, where the history teacher learns, through the course of his first year, how complicated is the art of teaching.[39]

People often ask me how I can get so much writing done. I tell them my great secret. Every day I put my seat on the chair. Every day. I work on what project is at the forefront, and I am always working on several projects at once. One day I work on an article that needs revising; one day I work on a poem from my Thoughtlog; one day I work on an essay; one day I work on this book; one day I work on a literature review for a study that we are doing. But every day I write, and I have done this for more than the ten years requisite for experts. It adds up.

Can a person be creative without a product? If you ask someone, "Are you creative?" and the person answers, "Yes," the next question is "what are you creative at?" The person has to give an example, or several, to illustrate. Thus the creator creates, within a domain of practice. So. Choose a domain. Something you have always wanted to do. Your "thorn." Now. Practice. When you get as old as I am, you will have drawers full, file cabinets full, of work you have practiced.

Ways Teachers Can Embed the Core Attitude of Self-Discipline

Here are some ways that teachers can embed the core attitude of self-discipline in their students.

Table 2.1. Ways teachers can embed the core attitude of self-discipline

Ways Teachers can Embed the Core Attitude of Self-Discipline
– Discuss self-discipline with the students and ask for their own hints and keys to self-discipline in work, diet, exercise, and various activities they want to master.
– Discuss long-term goal setting and short-term goal setting.
– Do a visualization where students project themselves into the future, see themselves where they will be in a month, a year, five years.
– Show and discuss examples of how people achieved goals.
– Break down long-term assignments into small steps, and monitor the steps with a chart, a list, and a personal high-five. Give students a calendar so that they can check off that they have completed the steps.

— Discuss frequent excuses that people make not to achieve their goals.

1. What's the point of all this?
2. Why bother?
3. I'm not good enough. I don't have what it takes.
4. Let's do it later.
5. I'll do it later. I'm going to do something else before I do it.[40]

— Have the students create a schedule for when they will do their work.

— Emphasize the importance of being on time for appointments. (If you don't show up, for the rehearsal, you can't practice.)

— Treat work as practice, not as a final product.

— Value hard work—emphasize the process, not the product.

MY THOUGHTS AND INSIGHTS ON THE CORE ATTITUDE
OF SELF-DISCIPLINE

Possibilities:

- Discuss how practice made for automaticity in the expertise you have acquired.
- How does self-discipline figure into your own creative life?
- Make an image (drawing, creative writing, music, photography, dance, diagram, skit, etc.) of this core attitude.

CORE ATTITUDE OF OPENNESS TO EXPERIENCE

Naiveté here means openness to experience, one of the Big Five Personality Attributes. An attitude openness to experience as a core attitude refers to the fact that creative people pay attention to the small things, and they are able to view their fields and domains by seeing the old as if it were new. They are able to view things as if never seen before, and therefore, they are able to pierce beneath the surface, and to make creative works that open up the field in ways that have never before been done. "Why didn't I think of that?" is often the reaction of other people in the domain. "I could have done that," is another reaction, but of course, without knowledge of the domain, they couldn't. This core attitude implies that the person perceiving has such familiarity with the domain, that the work can be done with skill and knowledge.

Examples from Creators of Openness to Experience/Naiveté

Examples abound in every domain of creativity. The invention of Velcro came from noticing burrs in the woods. Inventor Georges Mestral teamed with a weaver to create the fastener. Levi Strauss was selling canvas when miners told him they needed pants. When he made pants out of canvas, the miners told him they chafed. He substituted a fabric called serge de Nimes, which was shortened to denim. His knowledge of fabrics was essential to his naiveté.

Creators focus on the smallest details and probe what is beneath the surface. The photographer Robert Mapplethorpe and the artist Georgia O'Keeffe exposed the inner, erotic parts, of flowers, and people began to see flowers differently. The attitude is an attitude of acceptance and curiosity about the odd and strange.

The attitude of openness to experience includes the ability to notice and to remark differences in details. The artists Arshile Gorky and Willem de Kooning used to walk the streets of New York at night, pointing out the reflections of the few neon lights in paper thrown on the streets, remarking on the shapes and shadows, seeing the obvious as if new.[41] Composer Igor Stravinsky called this openness "the gift of observation." He said, "The true creator may be recognized by his ability always to find about him, in the commonest and humblest thing, items worthy of note."[42]

Poet Jane Hirshfield spoke of the source of the literary imagination as being perpetually perched on the edge, or in the margins. A certain receptivity is possible to people situated thus. She called them "threshold people." She said: "It is the task of the writer to become that permeable and transparent; to become ... a person on whom nothing is lost."[43] Hirshfield called this "threshold consciousness," where the writer surrenders normal conceptions of reality and being and adopts a new conception that includes the freedom of genuine love for "the many possibilities of being."[44] Keeping oneself in a constant state of wonder and curiosity is essential for threshold consciousness. One must view the world with naiveté.

One could say that cultivating an attitude of openness to experience is cultivating mindfulness, a Buddhist concept, but a person doesn't need to be a Buddhist to practice mindfulness. A person should just pay attention to the present. A good example of this attitude is often experienced when one travels. Entering a new city, a new land, the senses are open; one sees, hears, smells, touches, and tastes with gusto, and with curiosity, scenes and a milieu that the natives take for granted.

Exercise for a Group or for Staff Development

To cultivate the attitude of openness to experience, one exercise may illustrate. The raisin meditation is an exercise in being mindful of taste and smell. We eat, slowly, two raisins, noticing the taste, texture, and smell. The leader sits in a chair, demonstrating.

Put one raisin in each palm.
>Put your palms up in an attitude of openness.
>Sit in your chair, comfortably.
>Put both feet on the floor, your back against the back of the chair.
>Close your eyes and breathe deeply.
>In, 2, 3, 4,
>Out 2, 3, 4.
>After several deep breaths, with eyes still closed, and in silence, the leader says,
>Now slowly begin plumping the raisin that is the heaviest. Don't break its skin.
>Slowly bring it up to your nose, and sniff it. As you sniff it, feel the spurting of saliva from the sides of your mouth. Your body is responding to smell. Your wonderful body and its instincts and reactions are aware and open.
>Now put the raisin into your mouth and shift it side to side, without breaking its skin. Feel it with your tongue.
>Move it about, and, when you are ready, take a small bite. Taste the sweetness of the sun in the raisin bite.
>Now take another bite, but don't swallow. Slowly chew the raisin, enjoying its sunny sweetness, its fresh flavor.
>When you are ready, slowly swallow it, feeling it go down your throat to your beautiful stomach. When you are ready, take the other raisin and repeat the process, slowly and silently, enjoying the second raisin as dessert, being mindful of the process of eating. Keep your eyes closed after you have finished.
>When everyone is done, the leader says,
>Open your eyes.
>Silently, without speaking, write a poem about the experience.
>After everyone has written something down, the leader asks them to pair share, with a neighbor. Then the leader asks them who is willing to share with the group.

Other sensory exercises follow, in the senses of sight (draw a detail of this room), hearing (listen carefully to this music and to this noise), etc. After initial exercises in openness, and observation, group members keep a log about how they would apply this principle, this core attitude, into their own practice.

Exercises to Do Alone

To cultivate the attitude of openness, here are some exercises a person can try.
– Take a new route home from work, and notice new scenery and objects.
– Eat a whole meal alone, without media, reading, television, or music, with the plate in front of you. Appreciate the food's texture, smell, and appearance. Chew each bite 10 times before you allow yourself to swallow.
– Take a walk alone and pay attention to the sounds in your surroundings.
– Go to a museum alone. Wander around and when you see an exhibit that moves you, stay in front of it for ten minutes, concentrating.
– Do anything alone, take a notebook with you, and notice the Five W's of journalists: Who, What, Where, What, Why.
– Draw. Drawing is a means of cultivating openness, and the drawing is not meant to be analyzed according to skill. Many people, when asked to draw, say, "I can't draw." The purpose of the drawing is to pay attention, to appreciate the presence and purpose of the object, the scene, the milieu. Don't show anyone the drawing, but keep it in your Thoughtlog, look back at it occasionally, and marvel at how much you remember about what you drew by recalling.

Ways Teachers can Embed the Core Attitude of Openness to Experience

Here are some ways that teachers can embed the attitude of openness.

Table 2.2. Ways teachers can embed the core attitude of naiveté

Ways Teachers can Embed the Core Attitude of Openness to Experience/

– Create a climate for mindfulness: Allow time for students to settle in to the activity
– Develop an attitude of non-judgmentalism, acceptance
– Make sure this type of engagement is present in all classroom activities, in order to create meaningfulness.
– Slow things down and give students time to explore the little details.
– Don't provide an example; share an experience using sensory details.
– Since some children rush through things to move onto something else, do the relaxation technique and then have them draw an

object and commit them to a time (20 min/ half hour) whence only that activity can be worked on.

- Look at something from a different point of view—below, above, slanted, twisted, etc.
- Notice small things in sharing – children should be specific when they tell someone they like their picture, paper– they can tell exactly what they like
- At the beginning of a unit you could choose an object, a song, a picture, a functional piece that is representative of what is being studied and let their minds wander/or wonder about its purpose, function, meaning that is representative of the thing/unit to be studied
- Change the decorations, design, "set up," colors, textures, supplies, containers often. Ask children to notice what has changed to sharpen their sense of naiveté. Sometimes children are more mindful of their surroundings than we are.
- Create a game called *Private Eye*. Examine things closely–an apple, rocks, shells
- See connections between unlike things (synectics)
- Build observation skills–notice details, point of view
- Imagine all the ways this space has been used over the years. Imagine serious times, silly times. How were some of the ruts and holes in this old room made?
- Use the Invention Convention task to improve upon an object or create a new product explaining why improvement is needed or why the new product would be needed, focusing on details of the object.
- Daily or weekly notice the little details of each students' work, appearance, energy, comments and make a positive statement to them.
- Feel an object with eyes closed and connect it to abstract ideas.
- Have a child look at something commonplace and describe, "putting value" on things you usually don't pay attention to
- Bring in objects that are unfamiliar to the students. Play twenty questions on what the purpose of the object is. Ex: Old kitchen utensils.
- Have students see things in a new light by getting them to come up with alternative uses for something.
- Noticing the special/unique qualities of each child in the classroom, especially what brings them joy and how they express joy.

Science

– Observe the smallest details of nature; for example, draw the spots on butterfly wings when studying butterflies

– Look through a magnifying glass or microscope or the zoom lens on a camera, focus on and draw the enlarged image. And note the details.

– Scribe 1-foot squares. Describe what is within the frame.

– Examine a mosquito under a microscope.

– What would your view be like if you were an ant? A giraffe?

– Present scientific concept models and ask students to describe or explain the concept as they touch, smell, hear, and/or see the model.

– Use photosensitive paper with items in nature to help them see forms and shapes in a new way.

– Use *naiveté* to go through a simple experiment using the scientific process

Language Arts

– Write with an eye for detail, using sensory words and feeling words.

– Describe something by touch.

– Describe something common.

– Describe something by taste.

– Look at extreme close-ups (zoom books)

– Look at a common nursery rhyme. Examine what we know to be true.

– Dissect parts of speech. What do parts of speech *really* do? How is each dependent on a concept or an action?

– After reading a story, put artwork on the overhead and get the students to write what they see, and to explain what the artwork has to do with the story (art work comes with the unit).

– Before writing (middle school persuasive writing) have students reflect about how different voices and speaking styles influence them. Perhaps gather a tape of different voices saying the same short speech.

– Use exercises on "seeing" with sound, sight, taste, etc. to help students focus on details for story writing. Shut some senses down and enhance others. "Stories" need only be a paragraph long and not necessarily include the elements of a story, just detailed descriptions of sensory impressions.

- In writing memoirs, help children to "walk through" and convey the experiences they share.

Social Studies

- Bring something from another culture and ask how they think it was used.
- Imagine you are from a future archaeological dig. Find something in the room and make up a use for it. (Not its traditional use.)
- Taste the hardtack in simulation of a soldier's life.
- Take a field trip around the building. Who are these people in these photographs, trophy cases, etc?

Art

- Re-examine art for its concepts, perspective attitudes, traditions, etc.
- Draw something you are looking at without picking up the pencil.
- After reading a story, put artwork on the overhead and get the students to write what they see, and to explain what the artwork has to do with the story (art work comes with the unit).

Math

- tudents who test out of a math unit can look at the concept through "new" eyes and create a game that would require a demonstrated mastery of the skill/concept.
- What is 8 ½ X 11? Take a ruler, measure it on a surface, explore the ruler and the simplicity of the paper.

MY THOUGHTS AND INSIGHTS ON THE CORE ATTITUDE
OF OPENNESS TO EXPERIENCE

Possibilities:

- Describe how travel has contributed to your sense of naivete or openness to experience.
- Discuss how openness to experience has figured into your own creative life.
- Make an image (drawing, creative writing, music, photography, dance, diagram, etc.) of this core attitude.

CORE ATTITUDE OF RISK-TAKING

Risk-taking in creative people has been noticed since creativity began to be studied at the University of California at Berkeley Institute of Personality Assessment and Research in the 1950s.[45] Risk-taking enables one to try new things. While introverted and shy creators may eschew physical risk-taking, professional risk-taking in creators may be manifested in trying new forms, styles, or subjects. The kind of courage they have is the courage to stumble, fail, and, after rejection, to try again.

Psychoanalyst Rollo May called it "creative courage," which is finding the new, providing the vanguard's warning of what is about to happen in the culture, showing in image and symbol, through their imaginations, what is possible.[46] The creative artists and scientists threaten what is. That is why, in repressive societies, those creators who speak out in image and in symbol are jailed or exiled. They demonstrate courage in the presence of censure and rejection.

Examples from Creators of Creative Risk-Taking

For example, take the case of Nikola Tesla, the inventor of alternating current. He fought and won, fought and lost, trusted and was betrayed, and still remained steadfast to his principle that alternating current would eventually be preferred over direct current.[47]

The biographical literature is rife with examples of how creators stepped into the river of their domains and became, through the years, groundbreaking leaders through risk-taking work. Visual artist Alice Neel continued to paint portraits during the era of Abstract Expressionism, risking ridicule as a figurative painter, while around her in New York City, her colleagues painted abstractly.[48] The result was a shunning of her work. She did not get a one-woman show at the Whitney Museum of Art until she was in her seventies.

Creative writers, not known for their physical courage, are well known for their creative courage. What is the impetus for the coded telling of family tales, of private horrors, of straight-on traumatic memories, of needing to write it down? The true story resides in the place where one cuts one's own jugular, stabs oneself in the heart, slashes one's own wrists. Poet Anne Sexton, known for her frank confessional writing, was asked about why she dug so deeply into her own painful experiences:

> There was a part of me that was horrified, but the gutsy part of me drove on. Still, part of me was appalled by what I was doing. On the one hand I was digging up shit, with the other hand, I was covering it with sand. Nevertheless, I went on ahead. I didn't know any better. Sometimes, I felt like a reporter researching himself. Yes, it took certain courage, but as a writer one has to

take the chance on being a fool ... yes, to be a fool, that perhaps requires the greatest courage.[49]

Novelist Dorothy Allison, whose *Bastard out of Carolina* was a finalist for the National Book Award, also talked about the courage it takes to write close to what makes the writer most afraid: "The best fiction comes from the place where the terror hides... . I know that until I started pushing on my own fears, telling the stories that were hardest for me, writing about exactly the things I was most afraid of and unsure about, I wasn't writing worth a damn.[50]

Exercise for a Group or for Staff Development

The exercise used for practicing risk-taking is called "The Princess and the Pea." Take out a small piece of paper. List about five personal acts that would be risk-taking for you. You won't have to share these, so be honest and probe deep. What would be a risk for you to take? Here are some examples.

- Call your mother-in-law and say you're not coming over this Sunday to eat. Instead, you are your family are going to the beach.
- Tell your overbearing boss that a procedure can be improved.
- Try a new sport that you'll look like a fool doing, like golf.
- Change that hairdo you've been wearing for the past 20 years. Shave the comb over.
- Sing in a choir, even though your voice isn't the greatest. Choirs welcome everyone, as enthusiasm is required, and not talent. Since singing or speaking in public are two of the most feared activities for people, this will cut to the quick of risk.

Tear the margins of the paper so that only your list is visible. Fold this over and over, smaller and smaller, so that it resembles a "pea," and place it upon their body (in a shoe, in a pocket, in a bra, in your coin purse), where it will bother you and where you will notice it often.

Now, hold hands in a circle and look at each other. Take a vow to try ("I will try, Jane") to do one of the risks this semester. One student, whom I had the year before, came to me at a conference and said, "I took my risk. I finished a quilt and entered it into a quilt show. I didn't win, but I did it." This is a common result of this exercise. Each group meeting has a time set aside to discuss the group's progress on risk-taking.

Exercise for an Individual

Try something that would be scary for you to do. See exercise above.

Ways Teachers can Embed the Core Attitude of Risk-Taking

Here are some ways teachers can encourage and embed the core attitude of Risk-Taking into the classroom.

Table 2.3. Ways teachers can embed the core attitude of risk-taking

---

Ways Teachers can Embed the Core Attitude of Risk-Taking

- Create a classroom atmosphere that encourages the freedom to take intellectual and creative risks. This goes along with the core attitude of group trust. Students should discuss what such risk-taking means.[51]
- Demonstrate risk taking (Tell your own stories of when you took risks, similar to the stories above).
- Try a new sport together where no one will be a star, perhaps ice-skating, skiing, or golf. Have fun with it.
- Have students do self-assessments.
- Assign non-graded "process" assignments.
- Make sure students see the rubrics by which they will be evaluated.
- Use learning contracts.
- Use Thoughtlogs.
- Make a spot in your room the creative "safe zone."
- Do trust activities
- Give permission to be silly.

MY THOUGHTS AND INSIGHTS ABOUT THE CORE ATTITUDE
OF RISK-TAKING

Possibilities:

– Discuss how you or someone you know has displayed "creative courage," or risk-taking.
– What keeps you from taking risks?
– Make an image (drawing, creative writing, music, photography, dance, diagram, etc.) of this core attitude.

CORE ATTITUDE OF TOLERANCE
FOR AMBIGUITY

The term *tolerance for ambiguity* comes from the research done by that IPAR (Institute for Personality Assessment and Research) group in the 1950s. Historically, the concept of tolerance for ambiguity is related to the notion of the authoritarian character (Fromm). In extensive soul-searching after World War II, people wondered why they had submitted to authority, even when authority was doing such heinous acts as were committed upon Jews and others in the concentration camps. The thought went that people who needed leaders to tell them what to do were more rigid in personality, and they suppressed any doubts about the rightness of their government's actions. Intolerance of ambiguity was theorized to be related to just going along, politically.

How the idea of tolerance for ambiguity is related to the creative personality, is that the creator must be able to see the domain without firm preconceptions, and must be able to act without knowing whether the answer is "right," and without depending upon authority.

Examples from Creators of Tolerance for Ambiguity

Tolerance for ambiguity is necessary in order to not focus on one solution too soon. For example, abstract expressionist Mark Rothko would lie on a couch in his studio for hours and days, contemplating the placement of the shades and stripes and colors of his mammoth abstract paintings, rising occasionally to make a dab or two, mulling over the implications of these ambiguous forms.[52] As Allen Ginsberg said, "Nothing is black and white. Nothing."[53] Keats called it "negative capability," the ability to intentionally keep contradictory ideas in the mind.[54]

Likewise, psychiatrist Albert Rothenberg, who did extensive research on creators, especially creative writers, thought that creators used a Janusian process in creating, referring to the two-faced god Janus, who was able to face in opposite directions. Those who are creative are able to see perfectly well, both sides of the question.

James Simon, in a speech, noted that scientists who have authoritarian personalities are unlikely to make great discoveries, as they need more and more facts to confirm and are uncomfortable with tendencies:[55] "You have to be tolerant enough of ambiguity to be willing to speak or write without possession of all the facts." Theoretical physicist J. Robert Oppenheimer is a good example of this. He preferred to come up with ideas, but not to carry out the studies that would be required to prove the ideas; he left that to his graduate students.[56] Albert Einstein was described by biographer Walter Isaacson thus: "He retained the ability to hold two thoughts in his mind simultaneously, to be puzzled when they conflicted, and to marvel when he could smell an underlying unity."[57]

CHAPTER 2

Exercise for a Group or for Staff Development

Tolerance for ambiguity is illustrated through a discussion of critical thinking, and its various forms. Classes can conduct a mock debate about current issues, for example, the response to the New Orleans hurricane fiasco, with some people taking the role of Homeland Security, and others taking the roles of the politicians and mayor of the city.

Any issue where there is no right answer will do. People who want right answers when dealing with the improbabilities of life are often made uncomfortable when there is no right answer. They must tolerate the fact that no such answers exist, though there may be better and worse answers. The Gaza War in 2009 provides a case in point. Israel retaliated, after constant rocket bombardment by the Hamas Palestinians, with air strikes and ground invasion of the densely populated Gaza strip. Thousands of civilians were killed. Still Israel persisted, in the face of world condemnation and a rise in anti-Semitism in Europe and elsewhere. The result was a weakening in respect for Israel and a surge in sympathy for Palestine. Those who had been blindly supporting Israel, even fellow Jews, felt a deep sense of ambiguity.

Another strategy is to use the critical thinking strategies from the Critical Thinking Network in evaluating ambiguous material. In a course I teach, called Teachers in Film, students learn that there is no right answer in evaluating the image of teachers in popular culture films, and they talk about it in critical thinking terms. Here is where creativity results from critical thinking.

Table 2.4. 35 Dimensions of critical thought

A. Affective Strategies	B. Cognitive Strategies Macroabilities	C. Cognitive Strategies — Microskills
Table 2.4: Strategy List: 35 Dimensions of Critical Thought Copyright © Center for Critical Thinking, 1996. Used with Permission.		
S-1 Thinking independently	S-10 Refining generalizations and avoiding oversimplifications	S-27 Comparing and contrasting ideals with actual practice
S-2 Developing insight into egocentricity or sociocentricity	S-11 Comparing analogous situations: transferring insights to new contexts	S-28 Thinking precisely about thinking: using critical vocabulary
S-3 Exercising fairmindedness	S-12 Developing one's perspective: creating or exploring beliefs, arguments, or theories	S-29 Noting significant similarities and differences

Table 2.4: Strategy List: 35 Dimensions of Critical Thought
Copyright © Center for Critical Thinking, 1996. Used with Permission.

A. Affective Strategies	B. Cognitive Strategies Macroabilities	C. Cognitive Strategies — Microskills
S-4 Exploring thoughts underlying feelings and feelings underlying thoughts	S-13 clarifying issues, conclusions, or beliefs	S-30 Examining or evaluating assumptions
S-5 Developing intellectual humility and suspending judgment	S-14 Clarifying and analyzing the meanings of words or phrases	S-31 Distinguishing relevant from irrelevant facts
S-6 Developing intellectual courage	S-15 Developing criteria for evaluation: clarifying values and standards	S-32 Making plausible inferences, predictions, or interpretations
S-7 Developing intellectual good faith or integrity	S-16 Evaluating the credibility of sources of information	S-33 Giving reasons and evaluating evidence and alleged facts
S-8 Developing intellectual perseverance	S-17 Questioning deeply: raising and pursuing root or significant questions	S-34 Recognizing contradictions
S-9 Developing confidence in reason	S-18 Analyzing or evaluating arguments, interpretations, beliefs, or theories	S-35 Exploring implications and consequences
	S-19 Generating or assessing solutions	
	S-20 Analyzing or evaluating actions or policies	
	S-21 Reading critically: clarifying or critiquing texts	
	S-22 Listening critically: the art of silent dialogue	

Table 2.4: Strategy List: 35 Dimensions of Critical Thought Copyright © Center for Critical Thinking, 1996. Used with Permission.		
A. Affective Strategies	**B. Cognitive Strategies Macroabilities**	**C. Cognitive Strategies — Microskills**
	S-23 Making interdisciplinary connections	
	S-24 Practicing Socratic discussion: clarifying and questioning beliefs, theories, or perspectives	
	S-25 Reasoning dialogically: comparing perspectives, interpretations, or theories	
	S-26 Reasoning dialectically: evaluating perspectives, interpretations, or theories	

Exercises for an Individual

Avoid closure. Think about going on a trip. Do the legwork, but do not make final plans until the last minute. Note your anxiety level as the date looms. Tolerate it.

Avoid closure. Call people up at the last minute for a spur of the moment outing. Go.

Avoid closure. Do not do an assignment at work until the very last minute. Pull an all-nighter. Note your anxiety level. Tolerate it.

Ways Teachers Can Encourage the Core Attitude of Tolerance for Ambiguity

Here are some ways that teachers can encourage the core attitude of Tolerance for Ambiguity in their classrooms.

Table 2.5. Ways teachers can embed the core attitude of tolerance for ambiguity

Ways Teachers can Embed the Core Attitude of Tolerance for Ambiguity

General Classroom

- Build a climate that allows for opposing viewpoints
- Ask open-ended questions with no right answer ("What is good art?")
- Value opposing viewpoints and don't be threatened when students do have them
- Role-play ambiguous situations
- Start a debate society and make students research the problem, and during the debates, have them switch and argue several points of view. For possible topics, see http://www.middleschooldebate.com/topics/topiclists.htm
- Do the Creative Problem Solving process, as invented more than 60 years ago by Parnes and Osborn, where you alternate divergent production (brainstorming) and convergent production (criteria-finding).[58] See ww.creativelearning.com/CPSbookList.htm
- Have students list questions and topics that have no right answer.
- Read and discuss a novel, poem, or film. All good novels, poems, and films' plots require a tolerance for ambiguity.

CHAPTER 2

MY THOUGHTS AND INSIGHTS ABOUT THE CORE ATTITUDE OF
TOLERANCE FOR AMBIGUITY

Possibilities:

- How does your own tolerance for ambiguity affect your decisions?
- What experience with ambiguity has stuck with you?
- Make an image (drawing, creative writing, music, photography, dance, skit, diagram, etc.) of this core attitude.

34

CORE ATTITUDE OF GROUP TRUST

In collaborative creativity, which is the kind that is usually encouraged in business and manufacturing, theater, dance, athletics, and music, the people in the group doing the creating have to trust each other. Leaders make sure that the people in the group feel comfortable taking risks, being open and naïve, have acceptance for differing views and for incomplete answers, and that they do the work with regularity and discipline. From the raucous team in a closed room writing the jokes for a talk show or situation comedy, to the football team studying the game mistakes after losing the big one, members of a group must be confident enough and have enough trust in the process and in the group to be able to move on, to take criticism, and to do more.

Working in a group creates interdependency, as each member has a role to play, and a job to do, and they cannot be egotistical or selfish, or the whole project will suffer. One person cannot dominate; everyone must play and experience together. Trust is necessary among the members of the group. Each team or ensemble has its own culture. One must look for a "good fit." Creativity researcher Keith Sawyer called it "group genius," and he chronicled studies where the creative community had more juice than the individual.[59]

However, even when the creator creates alone, he/she is really not alone, for what I have called the "Sun of Community and Culture" on my Pyramid of Talent Development is operative; the work is judged by peers and connoisseurs of the domain; the creator socializes with and learns from other creators in the domain. No creator is isolated from the domain's rules, laws, and members.

The phenomenon of the "cluster," "a collection of related companies located in a small geographic area,"[60] illustrates the importance of group creativity. Silicon Valley in California, and the Silicon Fen in Europe are examples. These enterprises include research think tanks, educational institutions, businesses, and other forms of activity that interact and create creative capital. They are in proximity and the feed off of and nurture one another. The Silicon Valley, in 2003, had over a half million jobs at high salaries averaging $120,000, double that of the average U.S. worker.

Similar to the idea of the cluster, the idea of the "node" indicates the necessity for group trust. One person in the technological ether may create an attraction because of what he/she knows. The person may be anywhere, may be working in his/her pajamas, but what he has created attracts others of like mind, who gravitate towards his magnetic resonance, building upon what he has created in the techno-logical sense.[61]

Examples from Creators of Group Trust

The American Abstract Artists group in the 1930s gave each other problems at their meetings, as they experienced rivalry as to who would be the best teacher of abstract art, and who was the best abstract artist. Arshile Gorky would give them problems such as doing a painting with only the colors red and black, and they would vote as to whose was best. They would also produce a group painting and vote on "who was the beset draftsman, who is the best colorist, who the best in textures, and so forth."[62]

Mathematical creativity is thought also to be that of the individual. The mathematician sits in the think tank and thinks of proofs, scribbling numbers and formulas in the solitude of the ivory tower, and publishing the proof to the acclaim of the few other mathematicians who can understand. This is far from true. The mathematical community was shocked when number theorist Andrew Wiles solved Fermat's Last Theorem in 1994. He had worked for eight years in isolation, before he published it. He revealed his proof in a series of lectures at Cambridge University. Every day he revealed a little more. The lectures became crowded, as the mathematicians waited for the final proof, which came on the last day to loud applause, as Wiles said, meekly, "This solves Fermat's Last Theorem. I think I'll stop here." Mathematical genius Paul Erdös condemned Wiles as being selfish and glory-seeking because he did not consult with other mathematicians, and he felt that the Theorem would have been solved earlier if Wiles had done so. Even then, a mistake was found in the complicated proof, and Wiles had to have the help of a colleague, Richard Taylor, in order to patch the hole in the proof.[63]

Composer John Corigliano said that his musical friends inspired his work: "For the clarinet concerto, the inspirations were a clarinetist, the conductor Leonard Bernstein, a theatrical man, and my father ... who had been concertmaster ... For the *Pied Piper Fantasy,* the inspirations were James Galway."[64]

Exercise for the Group

Group trust in the creativity course is developed through affective activities, whereby group members feel that they can take risks without being ridiculed or teased. The sessions begins with a caveat based on the advertisement for Las Vegas: "What is said in creativity group stays in creativity group," to encourage confidentiality and no gossip about what people said. Each course meeting, group members must read their essays about focus questions aloud, and other members give them feedback. I also take group members on field trips, where they see and meet each other outside, and travel together, sharing personal experiences.

Another exercise to build group trust is to practice feeding back to each other through an exercise with fingerpaint. Fingerpainting levels the playing field, as everyone can do it. In creativity group, we first do a meditation. The tables are set with newspaper, a large piece of glossy fingerpaint paper, a paper towel, fingerpaint jars open and placed randomly around the tables, a bucket of water on the front table, classical or new age music playing.

Sit with both feet on the floor, your hands on your knees in an open and upward position. Wiggle back into the chair so you are balanced. Close your eyes. Breathe in. Out. Slowly. In 2, 3, 4. Out, 2, 3, 4. Quietly and regularly.

Listen to the soft music as you breathe. Leave everything behind you, your job, your family concerns, the traffic you had to fight to get here. You are here, now, and you are in a safe place, with your friends and colleagues. Breathe. [Here I pause for awhile, as they settle in, and breathe.] I am going to take you on a journey.

It is morning. You are walking east, toward the sun. [Pause.]

You are in a beautiful forest, on a path dappled with sun and shade, and morning birds singing and flying for breakfast. [Pause.]

The day is going to be warm, but it is pleasant now. You are full of hope and optimism, alone on this path, looking around you, delighting in the smell of the woods, the damp smell of earth and the soft rustle of the pine trees you are passing through. [Pause.]

You walk along, noticing your surroundings, in a state of peace and acceptance. [Pause.]

The birds tweet, and the trees move slowly in the dawn light. [Pause.]

You walk along the path toward the light off the water. [Pause.]

There, through the trees, you see water gleaming, and a beach. [Pause.]

You pause at the edge of the beach, noticing the slow rhythmic waters lapping at the shore. [Pause.]

Over there, you see a smooth rock, right next to the water. It has an indentation that will just fit you. You sit on the rock, remove your shoes, and put your feet into the cool water. [Pause.]

You are happy. Content. Peaceful. You sit, watching the sun rise, watching the waves lap, and think about the things that have been rising within you for the past few days. [Pause.]

An image arises as you contemplate here. This is an image from within you. It comes from your innermost self, and it has a clue, an answer, an insight, to what you need. [Pause.]

Hold that image and send it to your fingers. [Pause.]

Open your eyes and begin to paint. You may not speak to anyone while you do this, but be alone within the group, painting. If you need to begin again, there is more paper. When you finish, sit quietly listening to the music, and do not talk. Pull out your thoughtlog and write some thoughts while waiting.

When everyone is done, call for an art show. Rise up and quietly circle the room, studying each other's works. Then give each other feedback, according to the feeding back rules.[65] "We are going to consider each art piece, one by one. As adults, and as teachers, we are charged with judging student work. We give grades. We correct grammar. We give report cards. We are trained to judge people. This exercise is going to be difficult, because we are not going to judge, we are going to feed back. Don't say, "Awesome, dude!" or "You are so talented." Or "I couldn't do anything like that." Or "I think it's unclear what you're getting at." Those are all judging responses, or responses that lead to rulings. Instead, you must feed back. Begin your statements with any of these prompts.

Table 2.6. Feeding-back prompts

Feeding back Prompts for Reacting to Work[66]
1. This reminds me of ...
2. Give a descriptive adjective ...
3. I thought of ...
4. The work resembles ...
5. I see –
6. Awe—silence.

Pin each painting to the bulletin board, gather round in chairs, and each person take a turn, feeding back to the painter. Then the painter may speak about his or her intentions in the work. Take your painting home, and put it on the floor by your chair tonight while you watch television, study it, and remember what people said, reflecting on what you heard. Often great insight has been given to you from a fellow's comment. Group members often frame their paintings. I have done this exercise with over a thousand adults, and the experience is quite extraordinary for all of us. We end up with a feeling of trust, having experienced the loving concern and regard of our colleagues. When one does not feel judged, trust arises.

Here are comments from group members: "Not judging is a wonderful feeling! We are judged everywhere we go." "Not being judgmental is difficult, especially when making judgment is so much of what we do." "It was refreshing to release myself from the first typical reaction—like or dislike." "The idea of "feeding back"—instead of feedback suggests that we are all nourished by observing the work. Giving "food" or digested opinion—like comment back to the author suggests more of a reciprocal relationship. More of a two way continuum than a dead end street."

Exercise for the Individual

Join a group that focuses on the area of creativity where you want to work. If it's geology, join the rock hounds. If it's skiing, join the ski club. If it's mathematics, find the few others who enjoy solving proofs also. Men seem to have an edge in varieties of hobbies. As a person who has been long single and dated many, I have delighted in the fact that men have odd hobbies and they take you along with them while they practice. My oddest was the guy who was a hang glider pilot. He liked to crouch on top of high hills, listening to the weather on a short wave radio, talking with other loners like he, men in hiking boots and jeans, with plaid shirts, glasses, and the desire to run off hilltops and sand dunes with huge silken wings above them. I used this experience in my comic novel, *The Three-Week Trance Diet*, where the characters have a hang-gliding contest.[67]

Take a course from adult education in something in which you're interested. Building birdhouses on a bluebird trail in the local public forest? Do it. Birders are among the most passionate people around, and you can go on great hikes early in the morning, pointing your binoculars at trees and scanning bird books, making additions to your life list. Read the newspaper and find out where such groups meet. Check online. Do not be shy. You might think you are alone in your passion, but you are not.

Ways Teachers can Embed the Core Attitude of Group Trust

Here are some ways that teachers can encourage this core attitude, that of Group Trust.

Table 2.7. Ways teachers can embed the core attitude of group trust

Ways Teachers can Embed the Core Attitude of Group Trust[68]
– Establish a code of behavior in your classroom. It is a code developed by the group early in its existence, and not imposed from above.
– Model supportive behavior. Students will imitate you.
– Only discuss group issues in group discussions.
– Practice giving feedback (see above) that is not judgmental.
– Practice making positive comments about individuals.
– When a pattern of negative social behavior starts to develop, immediately act to change that pattern by taking the person aside and discussing it with him/her privately.
– When instructing or facilitating discussions, use the student's names, and sincerely compliment individual participants on their contribution to raise the general level of self and other respect.

MY THOUGHTS AND INSIGHTS ON THE CORE ATTITUDE
OF GROUP TRUST

Possibilities:

- Describe a time when a lack of group trust stifled your creativity.
- Describe a time when group trust enhanced your creativity.
- Make an image (drawing, creative writing, music, photography, dance, diagram, etc.) about group trust.

Reprise

These Five Core Attitudes may be modified and elaborated upon in any ways you want. They are not set in stone, either; I began with four core attitudes, then added tolerance for ambiguity, and may add others. But, revisions aside, at least these are essential for the creator to practice.

Remember, unless you want to, you won't. MOTIVATION is the key. I too am bored and exasperated by how-to books, so much so that I walk faster and don't browse when I pass the self-help section in the bookstore. But if you want to, try a few of the above exercises. Only if you want to—be more creative—cultivate the five core attitudes in your life.

SUMMARY OF KEY POINTS

1. The Core Attitude of Self-discipline requires constant and regular practice in the creativity area in which a creative person want to work.
2. The Core Attitude of Naiveté, or Openness to Experience requires that a person notice the small things, pause, and reflect, and open the senses to the world.
3. The Core Attitude of Risk-taking requires that a person take a few chances, and venture into new territory in the creativity area, that he or she tries new and perhaps scary things.
4. The Core Attitude of Tolerance for Ambiguity requires that a person not foreclose on solutions to problems, and realizes that there are no right answers, only temporary best answers.
5. The Core Attitude of Group Trust requires that the leader and the group practice respect for each other, with no snideness or put-downs.
6. Each of these core attitudes has been practiced by real creators, and can be practiced by a group, an individual, and by teachers seeking to embed creativity into the curriculum.

THE SEVEN I'S

Inspiration

Creators in the arts, sciences, education, and business speak about how they create in terms that I have broken down into the Seven I's: several types of (1) Inspiration, (2) Imagery, (3) Imagination, (4) Intuition, (5) Insight, (6) Incubation, and (7) Improvisation. I have developed exercises for each of these so that my students can themselves teach them in their classes and practice them in their lives. Inspiration has many types and forms, and so I will devote a whole chapter to the "I" of Inspiration.

THE "I" OF INSPIRATION

All creators talk about inspiration. Literally, inspiration is a taking in of breath. In terms of creativity, inspiration provides the motivation to create. Inspiration is a breathing or infusion into the mind or soul of exaltation. The word connotes the spiritual, and is deemed essential for creators. Plato discussed inspiration in at least five of his dialogues.[69] Writer and editor Stephen Berg said of it,

> The creative act is one of the most mysterious of all human activities. There is, in fact, an aspect of creating that can only be accounted for by a notion such as inspiration. Writers and artists know better than anyone that the phenomenon of inspiration is essentially impossible to explain, and that no amount of critical theorizing or introspection will account for the mysterious sources and transformations of their imagination.[70]

Composer Roger Sessions called inspiration "the impulse which sets creation in movement" and "the energy which keeps it going."[71] One of my students commented on the energy that ensues when teaching is inspirational: "Creativity is reciprocal. The exchange of energy that occurs when my students are creative fuels me. Yet it makes every mundane activity all the more frustrating."[72] The creator knows with certainty when he or she is inspired. Inspiration dominates and absorbs, and the person is unable to focus on other things. It may begin with a vague idea that may be very indefinite, but which has authority and emotion. Creators often see this idea as a vision that is attractive and powerful. The creator might not know what the inspiration means, but may take notes of it, or mark it, and return to it later. The force of the inspiration creates an energy that cannot be forgotten.

Polish poet Wislawa Szymborska in her acceptance speech for the Nobel prize said that inspiration is not only for poets or artists, but that inspiration "visits" people who know what their calling is. Inspiration helps them see the work as a journey, where curiosity triumphs even when they experience problems. "A swarm of new questions emerges from every problem that they solve. Whatever inspiration is, it's born from a continuous "I don't know."[73]

Creators in domains discuss several types of inspiration; among these the inspiration from love, from nature, from the transpersonal, through substances, from others' works, from dreams, from travel, from tragedy, from shame, and from a need for justice, among others.

THE INSPIRATION OF LOVE: THE VISITATION OF THE MUSE

Being inspired by regard for another—by the gaze of desire—has historically been called the visitation of the muse. Muse originally meant "reminder." The Nine Greek mythological Muses were inspirations for creators in various domains. Each muse had her own province in music, literature, art, and science. Calliope was the muse of epic poetry; Lyric poetry had Clio (remember the painting of Clio, *The Allegory of Painting* by Johannes Vermeer?), Euterpe inspired tragedy. Thalia inspired comedy. Melpomene inspired choral singing. Terspichore inspired dance. Polyhymnia inspired poetry celebrating the divine. Erato was the muse of love poetry, and Urania, the music of the spheres, of astronomy and astrology.

Examples from Creators of the Inspiration of Love

The person experiencing the inspiration of the muse is inspired by feeling, and seeks to impress the object of desire, by making something or showing something. The whole industry of greetings related to Valentine's Day, February 14, is an example of the pervasive inspiration of love. One need only casually study art history to see the myriads of works dedicated to desire. The paintings of Jean-Lyon Gérome (the Pygmalion and Galatea series) Cosmé Tura, Nicolas Poussin, of Marc Chagall (*Apparition: Self Portrait with Muse*), of Pablo Picasso's many models and several wives; of Salvatore Dali—the list is infinite.

This idea is an ancient one, with a broad classical literature that is seldom referred to by psychologists working on the creative process. The Platonic view is that the work comes from elsewhere than the intellect. The surrealists elaborated on this idea to theorize that the inspiration is from the unconscious, the unknown within. Jacques Maritain contrasted the Platonic and the Surrealistic views of what happens during the creative process: "The [Platonic] myth of the Muse signifies that the source [of the creative work] is separate from the human intellect, outside of it, in the transcendent eternal fatherland of subsisting Ideas." The surrealistic view is that inspiration of the creative work comes from the Freudian unconscious, from within: "there are two kinds of unconscious ... the preconscious of the spirit in its living springs, and the unconscious of blood and flesh, instincts, tendencies, complexes, repressed images and desires, traumatic memories, as constituting a closed or autonomous dynamic whole."[74] One source is outside, in a spiritual realm; the other is inside, in a psychological realm.[75] Thus, "visitation" of the Muse.

Listening to popular songs also illustrates the power of desire and erotic love to inspire songwriters. The desire inspires longing and the longing leads to the creative work. Take a look at the titles on your iPod and note how dominant the topic of love is in the titles and lyrics that you listen to. Songwriter Tori Amos spoke about the visitation of the muse thus: "You can begin to feel a presence when she comes. I call it a she, like it's a bath product. I would start to know when she's coming. And when that happens, I know I have to remember it. I'll write on my hand or something." However, songwriter and musician Dave Matthews said to Amos' description, "I get similar visitations often when I'm having a crap ... . Or driving, or something like that. I have these ideas and they come in and I'm, oh, very excited about them. But then they vanish." [76]

Poet Anne Waldman noted, "As a woman poet seeking Muse, I touch the woman in the man in myself." [77] Muses are virginal, pure, and faithful. The artist longs for the muse, and in the process of longing, creates a song, a play, a poem, a theorem. Inspiration by the muse also has a mystical aspect. The people who are inspired often say that they are possessed.

Classical musicians also speak of the muse. Composer Shulamith Firestone knew that there is more to creativity than the muse's visitation:

> Some people say to me, "Oh, you're an artist, you must have suffered an awful lot," and others say, "You're an artist—how wonderful it must be to have the muse come visit you, to just sit down and have these things happen!" Well, both are equally fallacious points of view. I think there is a muse, actually, but you have to make it come visit you —you have to find a way to invite it, and then find a way to work with it. Again, it comes down to discipline—the huge amount of work required to persevere and follow a vision.[78]

Exercise for the Group or for Staff Development

When teaching about the inspiration of love for creativity, discuss the Greek terms for love, which make for a broader definition. Often when the word *love* is mentioned, people think in sexual terms. The Greeks had several different ways of speaking of love–*agape* (love of God), *storge* (love of family), *filios* (brotherly love), *eros* (sexual love) and *patrios* (love of country or tribe).

A good way to insert some academic rigor and to simultaneously go for feeling, is to write a sonnet. The 14-line sonnet imitates human breath through the meter of iambic pentameter. Group members write a love sonnet, focusing on one or more of the Greek types of love. Since all talk of love incites emotion, and emotion is rather difficult to express, group members sculpt a holder for this powerful love, out of clay, expressing their love in another image—not words, this time, but earth. Clay is ground, earth, a way to contain strong emotion.

Exercise for the Individual

When you think about that certain someone, make something concrete—a poem, a song, a carpentry project, a food dish to contain your obsession. Now, if you have the guts, give it to him/her.

Ways Teachers can Embed the Inspiration of Love into the Classroom

Here are some ways that teachers can embed the inspiration of love into their curriculum.

Table 3.1. Ways teachers can embed the inspiration of love

Ways to Embed the Inspiration of Love into the Curriculum

General Classroom

– Show mutual respect to students – be a loving person.
– The students could generate music, poems, writings, of songs and advance those ideas into action – taking care of the building, treating schoolmates with respect, random acts of kindness, etc.
– Discuss love in relation to time.
– The talk show. Panel topic: How do you know if someone loves you?
– Allow students to work with clay especially when dealing with loss of loved ones.
– Teach your students about the types of love (agape, eros, filios).
– Teach them (especially boys) that it is OK to tell someone you love them, whether it be a family member, a friend, or significant other.
– Discuss love, what is real love, true love, etc.
– Identify facets of love for parents, grandparents, and friends.
– Have students describe the ideal life partner.

Language Arts

– Have students journal about love.
– Have students write a song or poem about love.
– Read love poems.
– Write a letter to someone you love.
– Write your own epic love story (as dramatically as possible). Compare love of family with "true love."

- What does love look like, smell like, taste like, sound like, feel like – write poetry about it afterwards.
- Use sonnet writing to help children get in touch with their feelings.
- Share meaningful picture books about love: Thank you Mr. Falker; Patricia Polacco books (she uses family tales). Have students share meanings or do a write off of an idea. Relate text to self, to other text, to world. Pose: How would the world change with love of all cultures?
- Do a writing assignment about a person who has influenced them in some way.
- Write an acrostic poem of feelings love brings.
- Write poetry in response to a unit that about man's inhumanity to man. Find examples of hope and love in places where they are not easily found. Create hope and love via sculpture, poetry, music, art.
- When teaching Shakespeare, love always pops up. Write sonnets when studying Shakespeare.

Arts

- Make a collage about things/people you love.
- Make valentines in November– write all the things you want to be sure that someone knows about how you feel?
- Paint, act, sing, your self-definition of love.

Science

- Use clay in science class. The kids could create how they feel about nature and animals. Many times children miss opportunities of how to truly love animals and in knowing how to treat animals respectfully.

CHAPTER 3

MY THOUGHTS AND INSIGHTS ABOUT THE INSPIRATION OF LOVE

Possibilities:

- Describe a time when the muse visited you.
- Describe how the Greek definitions of types of love resonate with you, with examples of each.
- Make an image (drawing, creative writing, music, photography, dance, diagram, skit, etc.) of the inspiration of love.

THE INSPIRATION OF NATURE

The inspiration of the natural world, from mountains, plains, animals, landscapes, insects, snakes, and all things natural pervades much creative work, and creators are frank in their gratitude to nature. Creators in all domains are inspired by nature. One of the most telling differences between scientists and mathematicians is that scientists are inspired by the opportunity to solve mysteries of nature, while mathematicians are inspired to solve theorems and abstract problems that nature presents. Mathematics is a tool for scientists, a tool which helps them understand nature.

Examples from Creators of the Inspiration of Nature

The inspiration of nature was particularly pervasive in the works of the nineteenth century British and American transcendentalists and romantics, writers such as Wordsworth, Coleridge, Shelly, Byron, Emerson, Dickinson, and Thoreau. They decried the industrial revolution and sought to return to simpler times when nature was pre-eminent, and not the conquering of nature. The artistic prodigy William Turner, said, "When I was a boy I used to lie on my back for hours watching the skies, and then go home and paint them; and there was a stall in the Soho Bazaar where they sold drawing materials and they used to buy my skies."[79]

More recently, songwriter and poet Bob Dylan spoke of how nature inspires him to write songs: "Environment affects me a great deal. A lot of the songs were written after the sun went down. And I like storms; I like to stay up during a storm. I get very meditative sometimes, and this one phrase was going through my head: Work while the day lasts, because the night of death cometh when no man can work." [80]

John James Audubon, the French immigrant who revolutionized ornithology with his drawings and paintings of birds and wildlife in the early 19th century, was so inspired by nature that he neglected his job, his family, and his friends, as he tramped the woods, observing birds in the wild, collecting and posing species, hunting, fishing, and capturing species, making mathematical calculations about them. Once he found a hollow sycamore tree into which hordes of swallows disappeared. He bored a hole into the bottom of the tree and burrowed into depths of feces and decayed feathers, to observe the sleeping swallows, taking measurements that indicated that 35 swallows could sleep within a one-square foot span. He then shot several, and posed them for his painting of the chimney swift. During his time, passenger pigeons, now extinct, flew in migrations that darkened the sun. He calculated that a flock he observed had two billion birds.[81]

Nikola Tesla, the inventor, stated that his purpose was to "harness the energies of nature to the service of man."[82] Albert Einstein's father gave him a compass when he was ill, as a child. This gift instituted a crystallizing experience for Einstein. He began to tremble, and he felt a rush of cold air. He realized in a flash, that "something hidden had to be behind things." Isaacson said that "After being mesmerized by the compass needle's fealty t an unseen field, Einstein would develop a lifelong devotion to field theories as a way to describe nature."[83]

The visual artist family of the Wyeths were also inspired by nature. The patriarch, N. C. Wyeth, felt trapped into illustration, and was very successful at it. However, he wanted to be considered a fine artist. He went outside, to the countryside nearby Chadds Ford, Pennsylvania, and made a simple sketch of haystacks. "How I did enjoy a little study I did of a group of haystacks," he wrote. "I loved them before I got through. There are no horses running, kicking and snorting all over hell in it, there are no scenic mountain passes, raging torrents, soaring eagles or boiling clouds in it, just three or four silent haystacks."[84] His son, the first Andrew Wyeth, born in 1917, took up watercolor as a teenager. A gallery in New York City accepted many of these when Wyeth was only nineteen years old. In doing them, Wyeth was inspired by nature. He would go away for days at a time, staying outside. He would tramp the woods and fields with large sheets of watercolor paper that he had bought custom made, spread the paper on his knees, and with three sable brushes and a paint box, he would render sketches and paintings of the cornfields of Chadds Ford and the rocky bluffs around the coasts of Port Clyde, Maine.[85]

Exercise for a Group or for Staff Development

A meditation day field trip (with cell phones shut off and out of sight) crystallizes the influence of nature on human beings, as the creativity group silently walks in a park in solitude, with only cameras, drawing materials, and Thoughtlogs, thinking about things. During the opening exercise, they stand in a circle in the early morning dew, and read poetry by nature poets. The mood is set, and these instructions given. "This is your day to be selfish. You are busy mothers, fathers, people with demands upon your time, people and duties pulling you in different directions. This is your day to be alone with yourself, to be selfish. Enjoy it. Put away all thoughts of home, still all cell phones, and just take a walk in the woods." This is often the favorite part of meditation day for the group members. Many get their ideas for their individual creativity projects on this day.

Exercise to Do Alone

This is easy. Go for a walk in nature. Take your Thoughtlog. Sit on a stump. Listen. Smell. See. Feel. You will be surprised at how calm you soon feel, and at how intense the experience becomes, as you use your sense of naiveté. Think about your problems. Think about your creative work. Think about nothing. Hear a bird. Watch a squirrel. See the water flow. Scoop your hand into the stream and splash your face.[86]

Ways Teachers can Embed the Inspiration of Nature into the Classroom

Here are some ways that teachers can embed the "I" of the Inspiration of Nature into the curriculum in their classrooms.

Table 3.2. Ways teachers can embed the inspiration of nature

Ways to Embed the Inspiration of Nature

- Conduct class outside in the schoolyard.[87]
- Take students outside to look at examples of erosion.
- Discuss Howard Gardner's naturalist intelligence as one of the "frames of mind."[88]
- Study the schoolyard and, as a class, design it as a place for bringing the inside out. Perhaps create a seating space from logs, boulders, or other natural elements, a place that faces the woods nearby, fences that have student-made natural art on them, etc.
- Plant a schoolyard garden, or have plants and animals in the classroom that students are tasked to take care of.
- Stock field guides in your classroom, and encourage their use.
- Put bird feeders outside your school windows, and in the yard.
- Display nature photos and posters in the classroom.
- Do a themed scavenger hunt outside, relating it to an activity or book the students have read.
- Do activities with digital cameras or GPS locators, emphasizing the fun and technology available nowadays.
- Using the core attitude of naiveté, or openness to experience, have students choose a stone or a plant leaf and use all five senses in apprehending its unique properties. Then put all the objects in a pile, and have the students pick out their "own" object.
- Designate a "sit area" for each child out in the schoolyard. Revisit the area often, having students write in their Thoughtlogs about the changes and new observations they make in the area around their individual sitting space. Have them make a creative work about their observations.
- Take the class on a resident outdoor education experience at a nearby camp, and participate in the creative leadership activities that often take place in such settings.

CHAPTER 3

MY THOUGHTS AND INSIGHTS ABOUT THE INSPIRATION
OF NATURE

Possibilities:

- List memories of nature from your past and your feelings about them.
- Describe a time when nature inspired you.
- Make an image (drawing, creative writing, music, photography, dance, diagram, skit, etc.) of the inspiration of nature.

INSPIRATION AS TRANSCENDENT EXPERIENCE

Creators often speak as if what they write was sent from something within but afar. Inspirations "come." They often credit this to God, or to a spiritual force, and are often humble about the experience.

Examples from Creators of Inspiration as Transcendent Experience

As far back as 1900, French psychologist Théodule-Armand Ribot, writing on the creative imagination, noted three types of inspiration—mystical, feverish, and concentrated. Here is the example he gave of mystic inspiration:

> Mystic inspiration, in a passive form, in Jacob Boehme (Aurora)[89]: "I declare before God that I do not myself know how the thing arises within me, without the participation of my will. I do not even know that which I must write. If I write, it is because the Spirit moves me and communicates to me a great, wonderful knowledge. Often I do not even know whether I dwell in spirit in this present world and whether it is I myself that have the fortune to possess a certain and solid knowledge."[90]

Some creators feel as if they are go-betweens, mediums. Some mysterious force impels them, works through their hands, wiggles through them, shoots from them. This type of inspiration also applies in theater. For example, some actors speak of being receptacles for their characters' souls, of being possessed. Today actors talk about "getting into" character. Athletes talk of putting on their "game face," an oblique reference to the mask, echoing the masks of Greek theater. They often have pre-performance rituals for entering the state of mind necessary. This might include putting on their makeup, meditating, or being alone for a period of time.

Writers also speak like this. Descriptions of the creative process among writers often take on language that is spiritual, mystical. Take this comment by poet Dick Allen: "A sense of mysticism, a complete dissolving into wonder and beauty has been with me through my life. I remember always feeling nearly ecstatic in childhood. I had known I would be a writer since the third grade."[91] The inspirational act has been hailed, since time immemorial, as having its roots in the divine. Poet Gerald Stern views poetry as akin to religion: "My poetry is a kind of religion for me. It's a way of seeking redemption for myself, but just on the page. It is, finally, a way of understanding things so that they can be reconciled, explained, justified, redeemed."[92]

Poet and artist William Blake wrote,

> I have written this poem from immediate dictation, twelve or sometimes twenty or thirty lines at a time without premeditation & even against my will; the time it has taken in writing was thus render'd non-existent, and an immense

poem exists which seems to be the labor of a long life, all produc'd without labor or study. I may praise it, since I dare not pretend to be other than the Secretary; the authors are in eternity.[93]

Actor Sam Waterston explained how he felt inspired by the transcendent during an acting experience:

I had a revelation in the last performance of the play that ignited the whole character and illuminated it in a great flash right while I was standing on the stage. It was like an ecstatic experience... . Everything was working perfectly, and I wasn't thinking about it any more and suddenly, I had a sense of taking off. It was like flight.[94]

Depending on the creator's religious tradition, he or she may believe that the inspiration came from a personal god. Jewish immigrant abstract expressionist Mark Rothko said, "The people who weep before my pictures," he declared, "are having the same religious experience I had when I painted them."[95]

Composer Johannes Brahms, three weeks before his death, in 1897, opened up to the violinist and researcher Arthur Abell, about the source of his inspiration. Brahms had been reluctant to talk about it before, as he didn't want to be considered weird or strange.

When I feel the urge I begin by appealing directly to my Maker and I first ask Him the three most important questions pertaining to our life here in this world—whence, wherefore, whither? ... I immediately feel vibrations that thrill my whole being. These are the Spirit illuminating the soul-power within, and I realize at such moments the tremendous significance of Jesus' supreme revelation, "I and my Father are one." Those vibrations assume the forms of distinct mental images, after I have formulated my desire and resolve in regard to what I want—namely, to be inspired so that I can compose something that will uplift and benefit humanity-something of permanent value. Straightaway the ideas flow in upon me, directly from God, and not only do I see distinct themes in my mind's eye, harmonies and orchestration. Measure by measure, the finished product is revealed to me when I am in those rare, inspired moods... . I have to be in a semi-trance condition to get such results—a condition when the conscious mind is in temporary abeyance and the subconscious is in control, for it is through the subconscious mind, which is a part of Omnipotence that the inspiration comes. I have to be careful, however, not to lose consciousness, otherwise the ideas fade away. Spirit is the light of the soul ... . Spirit is universal. Spirit is the creative energy of the Cosmos. The soul of man is not conscious of its powers until it is enlightened by Spirit. Therefore, to evolve and grow, man must learn how to use and develop his own soul forces.[96]

This extraordinary and personal account by Brahms of prayer, of invocation, of trance, and of the inspiration of the transpersonal has been disparaged by some psychologists and critics, but I will let it stand here as it is what the stenographer who accompanied Arthur Abell on his interviews, wrote down.

French visual artist Henri Matisse built a chapel near the end of his life, but he refused to be buried in it, saying that the chapel was God's and not his own. He believed that his artistic power came from God, and he built the chapel in order to repay God for his talent. The design became an act of worship. He chose everything to submit his talent to God, so much so that he only took part in worship services there but once. He designed every aspect of the chapel, including the altar, the stained glass windows, the cross, the lighting, the robes, the containers. He said, "This is not a work which I have chosen, but a work for which I have been chosen."[97]

Exercise for a Group or for Staff Development

Gather at a place of worship. A local cathedral is great, but a small chapel is also fine. You might even try a sacred place outdoors, a vortex or cavern. Denomination is not important. Before entering, the leader passes out a sheet of poems that have been inspired by the transpersonal. The leader quietly performs the poems as an attunement for the group members. Poems such as "Christ Came Down," by Lawrence Ferlinghetti, "The Second Coming," by William Butler Yeats, poems by Blake, Donne, Gerard Manley Hopkins, Rumi, Tagore, quiet and prepare the group for thinking. Then they slowly disperse into the place, separately wandering, looking at the artifacts, sitting, kneeling, meditating on God.

Exercise for an Individual

Do this exercise by yourself. Go to an empty place of worship by yourself and sit there, thinking. Make something out of the experience. If you want to be inspired by God, wander into the myriads of churches that exist in all cities, that welcome the seeking stranger. Be alone and meditate.

Ways Teachers can Embed the Inspiration of Transcendent Experience

Here are some ways that teachers can embed the inspiration of transcendent experience into their curricula.

Table 3.3. Ways to embed the inspiration of transcendent experience

Ways Teachers can Foster the Inspiration of Transcendent Experience
– Emphasize that all people have spirit and soul, and that this should be respected.
– Organizations exist that teach tolerance, emphasize spirit, and focus on the whole child rather than on the intellect or the body. Investigate these.

- Remember that inspiration may come from reflection on a specific religion, but that the inspiration from the transcendent is about a core human characteristic, that people experience transcendence in many ways, and that such discussions in a classroom should never proselytize for any one faith or religion.

- Study the foundations of various faiths, and the works of art and culture that have been inspired by these faiths. Many primers exist.

- Visit an art museum and look at the spiritual works of art and culture that are collected there.

- Respect students' stories about their own transcendent experiences. (See Group Trust)

**MY THOUGHTS AND INSIGHTS ABOUT THE INSPIRATION
OF TRANSCENDENT EXPERIENCE**

Possibilities:

- How did this section resonate with you with regard to your own creativity?
- Why are people afraid of this kind of inspiration?
- Make an image (drawing, creative writing, music, photography, dance, diagram, skit, etc.) of the inspiration of transcendent experience.

INSPIRATION THROUGH SUBSTANCES

The use of substances—alcohol, drugs, herbs—has a long reputation (though some would say disreputable) within the literature on the creative process in writers, artists, musicians, and others.

Examples among Creators of Inspiration through Substances

Aldous Huxley wrote about the influence of mescaline; Samuel Taylor Coleridge about the influence of opium (he wrote "Kubla Khan" after taking it—see the movie *Pandaemonium* for a fictional version of the composition of this poem)[98]; Jack Kerouac about amphetamines; Edgar Allen Poe about absinthe; the seventh century Chinese Zen poet Li Po about wine; Fyodor Dostoevsky about whiskey; Allen Ginsberg about LSD; Michael McClure about mushrooms—peyote— and also about heroin and cocaine. Others were Baudelaire, Freud, de Quincy, Sir Alexander Cushing, Gautier, and Havelock Ellis. Actors and comedians have also used substances, some to the point of addiction. Indeed, the rite of passage nowadays seems to be a stint in rehab, or the refusal to go ("No, no no"—Amy Winehouse).[99]

The list of substances used could go on and on. The altered mental state brought about by substances has been thought to produce a sense of mystical creativity—to a certain extent. Before such studies became prohibited, researchers such as Timothy Leary and Richard Alpert (Baba Ram Dass) at such places as Harvard (the Harvard Psychedelic Project began in 1961) did studies with psilosybin and LSD, in order to figure out the reason that substances appeal to creators and to explore the mystical experiences such substances produced. Allen Ginsberg, a friend of Leary's, opened his address book and offered the substances to the writers Leroi Jones (Amiri Baracka[100]), Jack Kerouac, William Burroughs, Gregory Corso, the artists Willem de Kooning and Alan Ansen, and many others. Huston Smith, a well known theologian, also participated as did many psychologists and intellectuals.[101]

Frank Barron was also a codirector of this research until he left for the University of California—Santa Cruz. He said, "We see frequently in creative individuals … an actual desire to break through the regularities of perception, to shatter what is stable or constant in consciousness, to go beyond the given world to find that some-thing-more or that something-different that intuition says is there."[102] He quoted a painter, who said that the results of having taken the drug included the ability to get more work done. Usually, it took over an hour to get into the full concentration necessary to paint well; a long term effect of having taken the drug, made the time shorter and the visual intensity brought on by the drug helped him to see in more powerful ways. The drug seemed to destabilize reality, and to permit the creator to see the real differently—thus, *altered* state of consciousness. This permits insight. Those who have spoken of using substances to enhance creativity talk about a feeling of universality, of oneness, of sharpened perception, of intensity and of insight.

Perhaps one of the most omnipresent substances is coffee. Poincaré described how coffee helped him figure out some equations. He would try various combinations of formulas every day, while sitting at his desk, but could not make progress. "One evening, contrary to my custom, I drank black coffee and could not sleep." He said that this was the key. "Ideas rose in crowds; I felt them collide until pairs inter-locked, so to speak, making a stable combination .... I had only to write out the results, which took but a few hours."[103] French novelist Honoré de Balzac famously adored coffee as a stimulant to his work; he would eat a light meal, go to bed at 6, and then wake up at midnight, fuel himself with cups of coffee meticulously brewed according to special procedures he developed, and write all night long.[104] The examples abound, but one just has to look at the local coffee shop, where people with laptop computers sit—some of them surely creating as the caffeine wells through their brains.

Tobacco used to be omnipresent as a substance that fed inspiration. The image of the writer pounding the typewriter while smoke rings rise about his head is an example. Freud needed cigars to such an extent that he died of cancer of the tongue because of his need. Composer Fred Lerdahl also found tobacco conducive: "I do much better work when I smoke cigars, but I can't smoke them indoors, so when I'm planning a piece, I walk around outside with a cigar. I find the creative juices flow in direct proportion to the tobacco juice![105]

The partaker of substances must have enough wits about self to descend into the abyss to reap what is learned there, but to also be able to return and put it aside. The danger of turning from creative messenger to addicted body is great, and many creators have succumbed, especially to the siren song of alcohol.

Novelist Robert Olen Butler, in discussing the use of alcohol among writers, thought that the alcohol was mostly used after writing, because the writer, while writing truly, has experienced such emotions and probed such inner depths that the alcohol brings relief.[106] Aldous Huxley thought that taking LSD would inspire novelists and poets to see the universe in a more spiritual way.

Musicians, especially jazz musicians and rock musicians, are notorious for their use of drugs, especially marijuana, alcohol, and heroin. Some have persisted in creating even while addicted.[107] Charlie Parker was a heroin addict. Bix Beiderbecke was an alcoholic. Again, using drugs and alcohol for inspiration is dangerous. Marvin Gaye preferred marijuana. He said,

"I *stay* high. I respect reefer. If you're an artist, you'll recognize its creative possibilities." He said that marijuana helped him be able to listen to himself singing. "I've always listened to natural sounds—like gusts of wind or raindrops falling on the ground—and grass helped me listen closer." He had noticed that Rastafarian Bob Marley was able to combine the spiritual and the use of marijuana, and said, "I've had my share of smoky visions." He started smoking marijuana because he hated drinking because of his drunken father, and in order to be hip—"what else is there?" but marijuana. "Slowly you see the world through this fascinating filter, and slowly you decide you'd rather live your life stoned than straight."[108] The reality television show, *Celebrity Rehab,* features musicians and actors such as Jeff Conaway, Brigitte Nilsson, Jaimee Foxworth, Daniel Baldwin, and rock musician Seth Binzer, who have publicly admitted they would not rather live stoned.[109]

Inspiration by substances is a difficult and often illegal way to be inspired, and so I just mention it. Nevertheless, the presence of substances in the creative process is markedly present in the biographies of creators.

Exercise for a Group or for Staff Development

Attend a cocktail party or a wine tasting and see how the spark of noise rises after everyone has a drink or two. (Don't drive afterwards.)

Exercise for an Individual

Experiment on yourself if you are an adult. Try your creative pursuit with and without a substance. See if it is indeed helpful in creating. Chances are that it is not, and that, as Olen Butler said, the substance is perhaps useful in recollection, but not in creation.

Ways Teachers can Teach About the Inspiration of Substances

Again, being careful here is key. Don't be like Leary, who offered the untested drugs psilosybin and lysergic acid to his brilliant graduate students at Harvard, some of whom literally had their careers affected. One of Leary's graduate student named Neil Friedman told his adviser Herb Kelman that "basically all the other students were doing the drug with Leary and Alpert and had formed a bond. A band. And I felt some peer pressure to become part of it."[110] Remember that you as a teacher have power and to encourage substances to enhance creativity or one of the core attitudes, seven I's or general practices is an abuse of power. I come from a generation where classes were held at professors' homes and substances were present; the pressure to imbibe was certainly evident. Some of these professors were our favorites.

MY THOUGHTS AND INSIGHTS ABOUT INSPIRATION
THROUGH SUBSTANCES

Possibilities:

– Describe a time when a substance affected your creativity.
– Why are people afraid of mentioning the inspiration of substances as a source of creativity?
– Make an image (drawing, creative writing, music, photography, dance, diagram, skit, etc.) of inspiration through substances.

INSPIRATION BY OTHERS' CREATIVITY

Many creators are inspired by others' creativity, especially by works of art, literature, science, and music produced by others. This type of inspiration goes along with the core attitude of Group Trust and the Sun of Community and Culture on the Piirto Pyramid of Talent Development.

Examples from Creators of Inspiration by Others

Friendships between artists of different genres abound in biographical literature. Visual artist Romaire Bearden said "It's seeing finally the work of other artists that makes you want to paint rather than things from nature."[111] What inspires is elegance and near-perfection. If you know your own domain, you see the work of some others working there, and may ask, "How did he do that?" That someone can do so easily what you have been trying to do, inspires.

Cross-domain inspiration by others' creativity, musicians inspired by writers, writers inspired by artists, artists inspired by mathematicians, scientists inspired by film-makers. Many poets have written poems inspired by works of art and music. The term for this is a newly coined word, *ekphrasis*. Keats' "Ode on a Grecian Urn" is a literary example. Baritone Josh Groban had a hit reviving "Vincent," by songwriter Don McLean, about the Van Gogh painting *Starry Night*, to give another prominent example. Composers regularly set poems to music. Sibelius' *Tuonela* is an example, of a rune from the national epic poem, *Kalevala*, symphonically rendered. The Marimekko designers also use the *Kalevala* as inspiration for fabrics.

The Canadian artists called The Group of Seven made history by creating an art that was truly Canadian, of the Canadian landscapes. They were Tom Thomson, Arthur Lismer, F. H. Varley, A. Y. Jackson, Arthur Lismer, Franklin Carmichael, and Lawren Harris. Harris had studied in Berlin early in the 20th century, and then returned to Toronto, where his family was prominent. His return enabled him to re-view the Canadian landscape with naiveté, with new eyes and a sense of openness. A traveling exhibit of Scandinavian art inspired him to paint Canada, his own land.[112] He was also influenced by the postimpressionists being exhibited at Stieglitz's Gallery 291 in New York. An art movement called *synchromism*, which was founded by American artists McDonald-Wright and Russell, whereby colors were treated like sounds (similar to synaesthesia), also influenced Harris' work.[113] The onset of World War I and his brother's death led Harris to a nervous breakdown and early discharge from the army. While recovering, he traveled to the Algoma region north of Sault Ste. Marie, Ontario, where he experienced a spiritual reawakening that led him to paint local landscapes, unique to Canada and the north.[114]

They later admitted one woman to their number, Emily Carr of British Columbia, who also had a passion for painting and writing about the natural world of western

Canada.[115] Carr had previously felt isolated and persecuted. Harris called Carr "one of us," and though she was very frank and independent, he encouraged to her in her solitary attempts to paint what she saw in the West.

In physics, the Manhattan Project put young scientists Nils Bohr, Joseph Carter, Enrico Fermi, Richard Feynman, Hans Bethe, and J. Robert Oppenheimer, among others, together in a remote location in New Mexico, the boys' boarding school at Los Alamos, where they inspired each other to perfect the atomic bomb that was later dropped on Hiroshima and Nagasaki. Bird and Sherwin, biographers of Oppenheimer, said, "Wartime compelled some mild-mannered men to contemplate what was once unthinkable."[116] Many of these young physicists went on to win Nobel Prizes, and they populated the think tanks of universities and institutes for decades.

The collegiality extended to Europe, where Oppenheimer had studied with Nils Bohr. Some of the physicists working on the project were displaced Jewish scientists from Germany, and then later, in the cold war race for atomic fission, the U.S. recruited German physicists, and subsumed all political differences to the needs of science. An interesting historical fact is that many of these physicists were sympathetic to the left; that is, the union and Communist movements of the 1930s and 1940s appealed to them. Oppenheimer himself lost his security clearance during the anti-communist purges of the 1950s, led by Joseph McCarthy, because of his past support for these. He had led the movement to unionize the faculty of the University of California, and he had socialized and attended meetings with known Communists.

The myth of the lone creator is just that, a myth. In fact, most creators do not want to please or impress the world at large so much as they want to impress or please their peers who are working on the same types of creations. This fact brings to light the palpable and real influence of critics on creative fields. However, creators do not often create for the critics. Composer John Harbison called it *support*, saying that the creator doesn't compose for the audience, because the audience is only exposed to the composition for a short time, and "you're not working for the critics, for God's sake. You're working for yourself and whichever members of your community will live with your music at a substantial level, give you some degree of support. Support is a very multicolored thing. It includes the people who will actually tell you, in one way or another, if you're on the track or off the track."[117]

Creators in domains know who matters, who is doing the cutting edge work, who is admired, who is getting published, who is getting recognition. They are, on the one hand, envious (why not me?), and on the other hand, admiring of those who break new ground in their area.

Recent television reality shows such as *American Idol, So You Think You Can Dance, Can You Duet,* and the like, have featured excruciatingly embarrassing auditions by people who consider themselves to be singers or dancers with enough talent and background to become professionals. These people lack experience of having received feedback and the criticism of the professional community, and are often unable to take the rejection of the judges, as they stumble, sing off-key, and blindly assume they are able to jump into the field without, as they say, "paying their dues." In fact, no domain exists where higher and higher-level practice is not required. Each domain has its rules that are enforced by the domain's gatekeepers.

Even those visual artists known as "primitive" (unschooled) are judged and admitted to critical acclaim and higher prices for their works by schooled and influential critics and connoisseurs. For creators who want to enter a domain not to become aware and to follow the prescribed rules of the domain, is folly, for their chances of reaching a place of respect and influence are almost nil. Space does not permit an explication of the rules for proceeding in the various domains, but prospective creators must know these rules, which are almost always tacit. Creativity group is but an attitudinal, emotional, and illustrational venue; if a student wants to achieve in a domain, the thorn must pierce, and the schooling must be undertaken.

The Sun of Community and Culture in the Piirto Pyramid is an environmental necessity in the development of talent. Almost all creators formally belong to professional associations and groups dedicated to the pursuit of creativity in their domain of choice. That said, the creativity can also be what Csikszentmihalyi called "little c" creativity; creativity as an enjoyable way to live life.[118] But odds are, even the amateurs and Sunday painters belong to groups and follow the work of certain peers.

Critics in scholarly fields are called "peer reviewers," and breakthroughs in thought and research cannot be published or recognized without the approval of these. Likewise, creators who are not in the scholarly business, who apply for arts or scientific fellowships must be approved by judges, who vote on who should be funded. Grants from foundations, the critics, who are the gatekeepers of innovation, entrepreneurship, and creativity, often advise governments, even individuals. Rare is the creator who functions without their approval. I was laughingly talking with a friend and colleague as we were sharing our reactions to peer reviews. "Now I welcome it," I said. "Even with all the craziness and idiosyncrasy of some reviewers' egos inserted into the review, you learn something," she said.

Popular musicians also find such inspiration across domains. A book of photos and text, *Journey to Nowhere: The Saga of the New Underclass*, published in 1985, inspired rock musician Bruce Springsteen. One night Springsteen had insomnia, and he got up and found the book on his shelf. "I lay awake that night disturbed by its power and frightened by its implications." Springsteen then wrote the songs "Youngstown" and "The New Timer," for his album, *The Ghost of Tom Joad*.[119] Avant garde rockers such as the Fleet Foxes, Grizzly Bear and Animal Collective, have, oddly, been inspired by the music of the Beach Boys, especially their experimental sounds of their late career. Robin Pecknold of the Fleet Foxes said, "The Beach Boys' music soaks up all of America, from the sunny sound of Hawaii to the folk songs of the south to the intelligence of the north-east. In hard times, it's about remembering the romance of the country, and also about the power of the human voice to convey those emotions."[120] Artist Grant Gilsdorf, who painted the work that is reproduced on the cover of this book, said the painting was inspired by the movie, *The Fountain*.

Exercise for a Group or for Staff Development

Answer art with art. Singer/songwriter and high school French teacher F. Christopher Reynolds founded a movement called the ur-realist movement, where creators in various domains are encouraged to "answer art with art." When one artist, for example, writes a song, an artist friend responds with a sculpture, a poet responds with a poem, a playwright writes a scene, and the inspiration is continued through the symbolic and artistic work of friend for friend. In creativity group, such artistic responses of one student to another's work are common. Find such friends. Join such a group. Feed back to each other with kindness and caring, but also frankness and helpfulness.

Go to a museum, a concert, a play, and be inspired. The creativity group takes a field trip to an art museum, as our state is blessed with world-class art museums. Ohio industrialists endowed museums in Cleveland, Toledo, Columbus, Cincinnati, Youngstown, and in other rustbelt cities. The exercise is this. Attune the group before they go off on their own by having them stand in a circle, following along with a series of poems I have reproduced on a sheet of paper, with pictures that inspired the poems. Keats' "Ode to a Grecian Urn," Auden's "Musée des Beaux Arts," Browning's "My Last Duchess," and others. They then go out into the museum, separately, alone. The instruction is to find a work of art that speaks to the heart, and to spend at least ten minutes in front of it, and to write a poem about it. Then the group meets in a central place, and each person takes us to the work of art, reads the poem, and acts as a docent for the work.

The exercise is often profoundly moving. Years later, as I pass through the various rooms of the museums with the current group, I recall former group members' chosen works of art, and remember them with the insight their choices gave me about them—the basketball coach's choice of the Gutenberg Bible, which pages are turned once a week; the young mother's choice of the French Provincial room; the young woman who thought she would hate the whole day, choosing a Cassatt mother and child, and weeping as she read her poem and pointed to the details

Exercise for an Individual

Read. Write. Paint. Study. Dance. Invent. As you do so, you will find you are moved and inspired by the works of others who are doing the same thing. As a lone writer of poems that are, nowadays, seldom submitted for publication, I begin each day with reading Garrison Keillor's *The Writer's Almanac*, which comes to me online, and I savor the daily poem, written by others more famous than I, and I feel connected to other poets, other writers, and our common history.

Visit museums, where the muse lives. In every town you visit, try to visit the local museum. Local history is often fascinating; local people volunteer and collect. Our town recently featured an exhibit of old scrapbooks. There are even books published that list interesting local and little museums.[121]

CHAPTER 3

Ways Teachers can Emphasize the Appreciation of Others' Creative Works

Here are some ways teachers can emphasize and embed the appreciation of others' creative works into their classrooms.

Table 3.4. Ways teachers can emphasize the inspiration from others' creative works

---

Ways Teachers can Emphasize the Inspiration of Others' Works

- Besides the suggestions for a group, above, put students into groups and have them work in teams, appreciating each others' contributions in a formal manner. "When you made that suggestion, I got a great idea. What do you think?" (No put downs.)

- Have students look for inspiration from a creative work by a living creator, and then have them contact that creator with appreciation. Perhaps the creator will write back. This is not inspiration from equals, but it will create a memory in the student that creators are real people who can inspire.

- Talk about your own creative work and share it.

- Decorate. Posters. Sayings. Your surroundings. Your room. Your office. Stack your bookshelves with good books.

- Subscribe to Garrison Keillor's *The Writer's Almanac*, whereby a poem arrives each morning. Assign a student to read aloud the daily poem, and spend a few minutes discussing it. [newsletter@ americanpublicmedia.org]

MY THOUGHTS AND INSIGHTS ABOUT THE INSPIRATION
OF OTHERS' CREATIVE WORKS

Possibilities:

– How have the works of the people in your creative field inspired you?
– Describe a time when you came upon someone else's creative work and were transported.
– Make an image (drawing, creative writing, music, photography, dance, diagram, skit, etc.) that is inspired by someone else's creative work.

INSPIRATION FROM DREAMS

Dreams have inspired many creative works. Dreams often have personal meanings that solve problems that the dreamers are incubating. Dreams can also present images that entice creators to make their works.

Examples from Creators of Inspiration from Dreams

The Surrealists encouraged creators to use their dreams as inspiration. Freudian psychology had a great influence on the Surrealists. Both Freud and Jung wrote extensively on the significance of dreams. Freud believed that dreams are wish fulfillment and Jung asserted that dreams capture the collective unconscious—the primitive archetypes lost to us in our waking state. The Indian-born and wholly naturally talented, meaning unschooled and untrained, mathematical genius, Srinivasa Ramanujan said that his genius came in dreams from a goddess named Namagiri.[122] Sculptor David Smith said that dream images were "exchange" images; that is, even though he didn't "consciously use either signs or symbols … they've arrived in my mind as exchange images," that ism "dream images, subconscious images, after-images."[123] Einstein received an image for field theory from his dreams; the prophets of the Old and New Testaments were inspired by dreams (cf. the story of Joseph and the 7 plagues of Egypt); the list goes on and on.

Dreams resemble films, and filmmakers have used their dreams to inspire their works. Akira Kurasawa's famous film, *Dreams*, illustrates how he was inspired by Van Gogh's paintings.[124] Film director Ingmar Bergman said he got many of his film images from dreams. Though these are anecdotal, stories told by creators and others, published studies also indicate that creators have been inspired by dreams.[125] If you think about it, acting upon one's dreams in a creative manner takes a lot of follow-up. To lie there dreaming is easy; to translate the dream into a creative work is hard work. I know this myself, for many a night I have dreamed the whole plots of novels, which have vanished as the day set in. People dream music, as well, and many composers have spoken about how certain melodies came to them in their sleep.[126]

Architect Frank Gehry was remodeling his house after his children moved out, and he was obsessed with it. He had a dream that changed his design:

A helicopter crashed into a Zeppelin, and the helicopter had a woman in a pink dress — and my house is pink, pink outside—flat against the hull—and she came crashing down on me in the street, and I pulled my mother to safety. I realized when I woke up, that it was about my house, that I was losing it… I don't know why, it's kind of mystical … I cut out all the stuff that I was hanging onto, and after that, I slept.[127]

Exercise for a Group or for Staff Development

Join a dream group, or start one. In creativity group, group members are encouraged to begin to write down their dreams in their daily Thoughtlogs, and several dream interpretation sessions are held, where a student shares a dream. We use techniques from dream psychologists.[128] This is a lot of fun, and we get insight into each others' lives through a discussion of our dreams. We take a depth psychological approach, employing group work, drawing, and free association. There are four steps: (1) presenting the dream (2) associating from the dream; (3) amplifying, or interacting with the images; (4) animating the images.

- Tell the dream, using the present tense.
- Association. Ask questions about the images. What do you associate with [this image]
- Amplification. What would you say to this dream? Draw the images, sing the images, dance the images. What do the images mean in story and mythology?[129]
- Take the image and put it into your life. When you see the image around and about in the world, note it. Make a corner in your home where you keep the images from your dreams. Reflect on them.

Exercise for an Individual

Begin making images of your dreams. It's sometimes hard to remember your dreams, and some people say they never dream, but you do. You do. Techniques include concentrating before sleep, and asking your dreams to become apparent to you, keeping a notebook by the bedside, and taking a nap, where your dreams will often come unbidden.

Composer Claude Debussy said, "I have these marvelous dreams. And then I have to think about quarter notes!"[130] This illustrates that creative work is hard work, and the inspiration is only a small part of the process. Dreams should be taken seriously, though. As an extremely intriguing example, a lawyer friend told how his best friend was able to retire because he played the lottery numbers he dreamed. Such success aside, keep in mind that we spend perhaps 25% or 30% of our life laid out in sleep. Our homes contain chambers filled with slabs upon which we recline. Take advantage of it. Pay attention to your dreams.

Ways Teachers can Embed the Inspiration of Dreams

Here are some ways teachers can embed the inspiration of dreams into their classroom curricula.

Table 3.5. Inspiration of dreams

Ways Teachers can Focus on the Inspiration of Dreams

— Talk about dreams and have students tell their dreams and illustrate them or act them out in a theatre improvisation activity.

— Ask students whether they have had any dreams about the subject matter in class. If so, have them write or draw images from the dreams and discuss them. Don't require this, however, as many students will say they don't remember their dreams. The point is to respect that dreams do provide inspiration.

— Do research on the importance of dreams, and how dreams have been interpreted. This could be a science/biology project or a free choice psychology project.

— Discuss how movies and dreams are alike and different.

— Find a story about how a dream inspired a creator you are studying in class, and tell the story.

— Create a climate where students can feel free to be dreamers. One teacher has a poster of *Starry Night* by Vincent Van Gogh and has posted a black sheet of paper with a silver pen next to it, where students write down their dreams.

MY THOUGHTS AND INSIGHTS ABOUT INSPIRATION FROM DREAMS

Possibilities:

- What is your recurring dream and how does it affect your creativity?
- How do you apply or use the insights from your dreams?
- Make an image (drawing, creative writing, music, photography, dance, diagram, skit, etc.) of a dream.

THE INSPIRATION OF NOVEL SURROUNDINGS: TRAVEL

Travel makes it easy to maintain openness and naiveté. Being in a new setting, seeing new places makes everyone burn with the fire of apprehending what is new, novel. Often, the traveler awakens to deep insight about his or her own reality, his or her own life. Oftentimes, the subject of the creative work is the creator's homeland.

Examples of the Inspiration of Travel from Creators

Pablo Picasso and Juan Miró traveled to Paris and painted Spain. American writers and artists traveled to Paris in the 1920s and painted and wrote about the U.S., as well as Paris. The artist Mary Cassatt is an example. Her Philadelphia family lived abroad for many years. She studied with Charles Joshua Chaplin, copied paintings at the Louvre, and became friends with many French painters, most notably Charles Degas. However, she also used travel to inspire her, even when living far away from her homeland. While studying in Paris, she undertook a trip alone, to Italy, to study Correggio. She lived in Parma for two years, studying and painting. Later in her life, when she was 67 and thought she was out of ideas, she traveled with her family to Egypt, where they cruised the Nile River. Her brother became ill. The trip and his subsequent death transformed her. She said, "Only if I can paint something of what I have learnt may I be well."[131]

Travel has not only the advantage of fostering openness or naiveté, as the traveler sees with new eyes, that which the locals see with jaded eyes; it also has the advantage of distraction. Leaving the familiar, the workroom, the studio, the laboratory, the office, the husband, the kids, enforces a sense of rest or fallowness, which can encourage the creator to think anew about the work; that is, travel encourages incubation. Henri Poincaré, the mathematician, said, "The changes of travel made me forget my mathematical work."[132] The forgetting becomes part of the I of Incubation, described below.

This is even true for commuters, who, surrounded by with their favorite music playing in their cars, safely negotiating the lull of the freeway, in the isolation of the solitary commute in beginning the morning or finishing the day in the evening, create a space by which to forget, where ideas percolate through the sands of physicality and languourousness, to rise when the thought is done and the insight is needed. The comfortability of the incubation may be a reason why forcing people to commute in public transportation or to car pool has been a difficult task. That is not to forget subway and bus riders in urban areas, who retreat into sound and print during the crowded rush hours.

Novelist Martin Cruz Smith published what he called sociological novels fed by his sense of naïveté while he traveled. While traveling he took notes, drew pictures, and took photographs. He said,

When I start, I'm aware of the extent of my ignorance, so I naturally question everything. For example, when I was woken one morning by street vendors outside my hotel, I noticed that they didn't all arrive at once, but there was an order to it. Also, the sound was not of shoes on the street but of clogs. It was important. There are things you experience that are so basic that people just don't tell you. It's a little bit like people telling you about going to sea—nobody bothers to tell you that it is salty. They always overlook the details.[133]

I often feel inspired to write poems when I am traveling, as the surprises I am beholding tickle my sense of naiveté.[134]

Exercises for a Group or for Staff Development

– Tell a story about a trip you made. Recall how you felt when you first saw and apprehended the strange wonders of new places. Tell this with detail. Ask each other questions.
– Take a field trip with the whole group.
– Join a tour to a new and long-anticipated place
– Take a different seat than the place you usually sit in a meeting, an event, a group.
– Go to one of the cultural centers nearby.

When I have given workshops at various universities, I have asked the organizers to make an appointment for a group of us to go to the university archives or to the university museum. Locals often have never visited these "foreign" places. I remember about 50 of us hiking across the campus of Utah State University, Thoughtlogs in hand, to the university museum's exhibit of miniature boxes made by contemporary artists, an exhibit whose memory I treasure. I remember my young poets' group when I was principal of Hunter College Elementary School, during our monthly poets' lunches. We would walk down Fifth Avenue to the Metropolitan Museum of Art, new notebooks and pencils in hand, remarking on the towers of the fancy buildings across the Avenue, scrawling notes for poems. We would enter the Museum, and one child would pick the room we would visit. We would circle the room, studying the art objects, writing notes, making marks. We would then walk back to school. Once we had filmmakers from *Nova* with us, doing a show on child prodigies. We thought we would be documentary stars, but sadly, we ended up on the cutting room floor, with just a brief shot of us climbing the steps of the Museum, and a fast credit on the rolling end.

Exercises for an Individual

– Take a new route home. Notice the surroundings as if you are a person from a foreign country, seeing things for the first time.
– Take a trip. Notice how heightened your senses are, even when you are tired and scared. Take photographs. Take notes. Make marks. Talk to people. Go to a café alone and overhear what the people in the new place are saying. Take a walk and keep your eyes and ears open. Make sure to keep a travel journal.

The important thing about being inspired by travel, is to take notes, draw pictures, transcribe the notes, and download and work with the pictures, to use them afterwards. Anthropologist Margaret Mead promised herself to transcribe her notes immediately after every trip, and not to go on another trip to collect ceremonies and rituals of various tribes, until she had completed the notes from the last trip. After she died, she deposited 500,000 pieces of materials into the Library of Congress, one of the largest collections of materials from a single person.[135] Artifacts can also be collected; I collect road stones and place them on my window sill or in a sacred circle I have outside my back door.

Ways Teachers can Embed Travel as an Inspiration for Creativity

Here are some ways teachers can use travel as an inspiration for creativity in students.

Table 3.6. Ways teachers can embed travel as an inspiration

Ways Teachers can Embed the Inspiration of Travel for Creativity

- Talk about your own trips. Show the pictures. Tell stories. (Don't do this too much, though—personal examples are very powerful and should be used sparingly.)
- Have students talk about their family trips. Give credit for travel. Some parents pull their children out of school for travel. Take advantage of this and have the students keep a Thoughtlog about the new sights they have seen, and make a product about them, teaching the rest of the students what they have learned.
- Arrange a student trip overseas, and lead it.
- Arrange a student trip to a site in your city, state, or nation, and lead it.
- Send a postcard to each of your students when you travel. They'll remember it forever.

MY THOUGHTS AND INSIGHTS ABOUT THE INSPIRATION OF TRAVEL

Possibilities:

— Be particular and describe (re-see) a travel experience.
— How does armchair traveling (television, books) inspire you?
— Make an image (drawing, creative writing, music, photography, dance, diagram, skit, etc.) of an inspiring travel experience.

INSPIRATION OF THE DARK SIDE

The creative inspiration is not always pretty, safe, nice. Great creative works have been inspired by death, illness, depression, sadness, tragedy, mysterious goings-on.

Examples from Creators of the Inspiration of the Dark Side

The scary works of Edgar Allan Poe come immediately to mind. Poe himself had a fit beginning to help him produce such works. His teenage mother was ill and his father had abandoned him, his sister, and their mother in a hotel room. She had consumption, tuberculosis. Poe was a toddler. He and his sister, they figure, crept about the room with their mother dead on the bed, for several days, until they were discovered. What was the psychological impact of that pre-conscious memory experience?

Examples abound. Ludwig van Beethoven composed the Symphony in D major during a period in which he purportedly was contemplating suicide. Stravinsky wrote his Symphony in C during a period when some of his friends and family had died. Isabel Allende wrote herself through her daughter's terminal illness. She began a form of magical thinking. "I started to think that as long as I wrote, Paula would stay alive. It was a way of defying death."[136] The works that resulted moved many.

Psychologist Jock Abra theorized that creativity is enhanced when death is present.[137] He listed several aspects of this: creativity as a way to survive dying, through achieving eminence (Van Gogh sold only one painting but now he is the most expensive and eminent artist ever); creativity as a struggle with death ("Do not go gentle into that good night," as Welsh poet Dylan Thomas wrote); creativity as a way to symbolically render the meaning of death (expressed comedically in *The Bucket List* and more tragically in Elie Wiesel's *Night*); creativity as a way to deny death through repression and sublimation (fiddling while Rome burns); creativity as a way to comfort those who have experienced death (Mozart's *Requiem,* the AIDS quilt, the mobile Vietnam memorial). Creativity as a way to see what death is like (Houdini plunging, chained, into the icy river, people going over Niagara Falls in a barrel); creativity as a way to verify life in the midst of death (the birth scene in *The Grapes of Wrath*).

The wide outpouring of creativity after September 11, 2001, illustrates this type of inspiration. My whole network of artist friends individually responded, and we shared through our works. One friend began his song with the line "The children are weeping," as he described the students watching televisions in their classrooms in the school where he taught. Another made pots that were thrown into shards that became sharp points within an earthen grid.

Exercises for a Group or for Staff Development

Visit a cemetery. In creativity group, take a field trip to a nearby cemetery. To wander the tombstones in silence, is a profound experience. Scan the tiny flags waving for veterans of wars the U.S. has fought. Every area has cemeteries that reveal the local history. Begin the meditation on the dark side at these cemeteries, by an attunement of read poems by writers from the region. For example, in the Midwest, "In A Dark Time," by Theodore Roethke (who was a Michigan native), "Ode to the Confederate Dead," by Allen Tate (who taught at Kenyon College), "Island," by Langston Hughes (who went to high school in Cleveland).

The leader sends the group off to wander the cemetery silently, each alone with his/her thoughts, for an hour, and then all come back, sit in a circle, and share. This is a powerful exercise. The leader should caution people who are in the midst of mourning or personal pain, who feel they do not want to go into this experience, to just sit out.

A funny personal story might be appropriate here. Once we were in the historic Lake View Cemetery in Cleveland, Ohio on a beautiful spring Saturday. More than 102,000 people are interred there, among them John D. Rockefeller, James A. Garfield, and Elliot Ness. Joggers and dog walkers passed. The spring magnolias bloomed in profuse splendor. I was reading the dark side poems to my group ("Ode to the Confederate Dead," by Allan Tate; "In A Dark Time," by Theodore Roethke; "Island," by Langston Hughes; "Srebreniça," by Jane Piirto; "In Reading Town in Reading Gaol" by Oscar Wilde) and we were standing in a circle, heads bowed, as they followed along with me on the handouts. A van that looked like a television van pulled up on the road, and a man left the truck and made his way over to us. He listened, and then, as I sent the group off to wander with their thoughts, he asked what we were doing. "Meditating on the dark side as inspiration for creativity," I said. It turned out he was Rick Sebak, and they were making a documentary about what people do in cemeteries. They pulled out the release forms, and we signed, and they interviewed us and followed us about. We thought we were going to be documentary stars. But we were foiled. We ended up on the cutting room floor, but if you look at the fast running credits, of the PBS documentary, *A Cemetery Special*, you can see a brief thank you to the creativity group.[138]

Ways Teachers Can Honor the Dark Side as Inspiration for Creativity

Here are some ways teachers can acknowledge that bad things happen to people, and that these are often an inspiration for creative works. This is not negative; it is true. The climate of trust that has been engendered in a class can be accessed here.

Table 3.7. Ways teachers can honor the inspiration of the dark side

Ways Teachers can Honor the Dark Side as Inspiration for Creativity
– Be serious when teaching about the curriculum of wars and battles, about the sure fact that violence leads to death and suffering. A television show on the successful landing of an airbus on the Hudson River counted up the people who were in the families of those who would have died without the heroism of "Scully," the pilot.

There is always collateral damage in the heroism of war and violent accident. Make sure the students are aware of this. Have them do some research about it and give reports about it.[139]

- Conduct a field trip to a Civil War Battlefield such as Gettysburg, or other battefields nearby. These exist all over the world.

- Read war literature and memoirs of soldiers along with the history books.

- Read slave narratives.

- Read novels and Shakespeare's plays and Greek tragedies. All have "dark side" themes and scenes, as this is part of the dramatic arc.

- Research disease and do units on them. The College of William and Mary field-tested curriculum units could be a model.

- Have students research and debate both sides of a controversial question (see Tolerance for Ambiguity), as an exercise in critical thinking.

- Talk about the saying, "each dark cloud has a silver lining" in its reverse.

- Play protest songs. There are a jillion. (As I write this, my iPod shuffles to Lennon's "Imagine." An example of synchronicity.[140])

MY THOUGHTS AND INSIGHTS ABOUT THE INSPIRATION
OF THE DARK SIDE

Possibilities:

— Be particular and describe (re-see) an experience that was traumatic for you.
— How does your reading, game-playing, television-viewing, etc., affect your view of the tragedies in the world?
— Make an image (drawing, creative writing, music, photography, dance, diagram, skit, etc.) of the inspiration of the dark side.

INSPIRATION FROM BEING THWARTED

The "I'll show you" reason for creating is also a powerful one. Many have been told they will not create, they will not achieve, they will never make anything of themselves, and they internalize this and say, "I'll show you." Years later, the thwarter, the sarcastic teacher, the person who made the negative comment, receives an invitation to a graduation or to a party celebrating the creative accomplishments of the person who was thwarted. Creators are sensitive to criticism, but they combine that with remarkable persistence and resilience. I often wonder what happens to the thousands of young artists who major in and get degrees in fine arts as they submit their works and experience rejection after rejection—the mythology abounds with stories of writers who paste rejection slips up like wallpaper, of singers who go to Nashville and then return home, dejected, of actors going to audition after audition in between waitperson jobs. What do they do when, finally, they realize the world is not beating a path to their door, and they have to "settle" for that secure job at the insurance company? What happens to their creative spirit?

Examples from Creators of Inspiration from being Thwarted

Rivalries exist in all domains, and the "I'll show you" motive inspires creators, even those who are prominent and recognized as eminent. Biologist J. Craig Venter, in his memoir, *A Life Decoded*, described the huge rivalries at the National Institute of Health, among colleagues striving to unlock the secrets of DNA. He told this story.

> Scientific history is littered with stories of one person having an idea but not following through on it only to see another have a similar inspiration and then prove it to be valid… A proposal that cDNA clones from a fruit fly library should be randomly selected and sequenced had also been included in a 1990 grant application to the NIH Genome Center by Steve Henikoff of the Fred Hutchinson Cancer Research Center in Seattle… Steve had to go through the length process of writing a grant application and waiting nine months for a review. For his trouble he received a five-page critique citing all the reasons the method would never work and denying him funding. Steve sent me a copy after my paper was published in *Science* and told me that he posted a copy of the dismal review of his proposal on his lab wall, next to my picture and the *Science* article.[141]

The motivation for creativity that competition inspires pervades all domains. A researcher who publishes in a journal when the rejection rate is over 85%, and when the rule for tenure is to publish or perish, emerges triumphant over the competition and builds his or her reputation. Vicious rivalries exist in all fields, as the "I'll show you" reason for creating rewards and hinders creative efforts. James D. Watson and Francis Crick outrightly said that they were struggling to win the race for the rewards, such as the Nobel Prize, when they sought DNA's molecular structure. Watson himself said that competition was more of an incentive than cooperation.[142]

Picasso only wanted to be greater than Manet, and even in his 80s, in 1960s, he made a series of paintings responding to Manet's seminal 1863 *Dejeuner Sur L'Herbe*. Critic Blake Gopnik, in commenting on Picasso's "insanely competitive nature," even with dead rivals, said: "He quotes his ancestors only to outdo and out-shout them: When he's nearby on a museum wall, the greatest old-time picture can be hard to see. Picasso's imitation is sincerest flattery."

Entrepreneurs Helena Rubenstein's and Elizabeth Arden's rivalry fed their creativity.[143] They simultaneously and separately created makeup, cosmetic, and creams domains. Their fancy salons were near each other, and lived a few blocks from each other, and purposely never met. Rubinstein, a Polish-Jewish immigrant, and Arden (a pseudonym for a Canadian farm girl immigrant named Graham), were early suffragists, who saw the opportunity to create businesses serving the market of the young, independent women of the 1920s. Rubinstein collected 20th century art and Arden had thoroughbred racehorses. When Rubinstein married nobility, Arden did the same. They followed each other's careers and they made snide remarks about each other to the press while they made millions and influenced two generations of women. Both mistook the challenges posed by Charles Revson, Estee Lauder, and Avon Cosmetics, and their empires suffered. They went to their graves rich and still inspired by each other and hating each other.

Exercise for a Group and for an Individual

Think of a time in your life when you created something for the "I'll show you" motive. If you wish, tell your story. Or make an image that codes the story.

CHAPTER 3

MY THOUGHTS AND INSIGHTS ABOUT THE INSPIRATION
OF BEING THWARTED

Possibilities:

- Why should being thwarted inspire creativity?
- Tell a story about you or someone you know creating because of frustration.
- Make an image drawing, creative writing, music, photography, dance, diagram, skit, etc.) of the inspiration of being thwarted.

INSPIRATION FROM A SENSE OF INJUSTICE

Many philanthropic foundations have begun when people felt a need for creating a way to heal suffering, to do research on certain maladies, to help the needy. The creation of such endeavors is also creativity, and should be noted.

Examples from Creators of Inspiration from a Sense of Injustice

Michael J. Fox has Parkinson's disease. Christopher Reeve fell off a horse and became paralyzed. One child died, and another child became a quadriplegic after accidents caused by repeat drunk drivers. Alcohol had taken over the lives of Bill W., a New York stockbroker, and Dr. Bob S., an Akron surgeon. My cousin's husband died of a brain tumor.

Michael J. Fox founded a foundation for Parkinson's research. Christopher Reeve and his wife founded The Christopher and Dana Reeves Foundation for spinal cord research. Candy Lightner founded Mothers Against Drunk Driving in 1980 after her daughter, Cari, was killed by a repeat drunk driving offender. Another mother, Cindy Lamb, had a daughter, Laura, who became a quadriplegic after being hit by a drunk drive, cofounded MADD with Mrs. Lightner. Bill W. and Bob S. founded Alcoholics Anonymous. My cousin and her four daughters sponsor an annual walk for brain research along the shores of Lake Michigan in their small town of Escanaba, Michigan, and they give the proceeds to the Brain Research Center at the Marquette Medical Center.

It was unfair that these troubles were visited upon these people, and their sense of unfairness, about how traumatic it was that they had to suffer, and to be vested with such troubles, led them to create organizations that have done boundless good. While most of us will not have to become sick or have a horseback riding accident, or have our children innocently be victims of drunk drivers, or succumb to alcoholism, we have all created out of a sense of "that's not fair." The tinge of the personal and the desire for personal justice have been the foundation for many creative acts.

John Muir was the founder of the Sierra Club. His love of mountains, of long hikes, of tramping, of wildlife, and of nature, was being threatened in the late 1800s by relentless exploitation by miners, hunters, ranchers, and others who saw nature as a force to be tamed rather than as a bounty to preserve. Muir, a nature writer, naturalist, and stubborn native of Scotland via Wisconsin to California, became enamored of the great forests and mountains of California and Oregon, and, with friends, founded the Sierra Club in 1892. He was trying to expand the boundaries of the public park, Yosemite, by adding the Hetchy Hetchy Valley, to prevent the dam that went up there. His efforts helped persuade Theodore Roosevelt to designate other wilderness areas as inviolate.[144] The Valley did not become a part of the park until 1905.

Muir, a loner, came to see the value of group trust and unity. A group of people who loved to hike, led by Robert Underwood Johnson, a San Francisco attorney, and Warren Olney, began a defense league focused on preserving the new Yosemite Park. They incorporated and Muir was overwhelmingly elected president. The rest is history.

The earthquake in Haiti in 2010 brought forth a stream of groups, foundations, and television special where creators donated their time and efforts to raise funds to help the poor nation rise from the rubble. The better-off nation of Chile, which also experienced a massive earthquake, at first refused aid, and then accepted it, but the hearts of the world went out to the poorer nation. The "We Are The World" group reconstituted itself and projected deceased Michael Jackson into the group in a time traveling way, while they re-recorded the song as a charity donation, available for download from iTunes.

Exercise for a Group or for Staff Development

Discuss what makes you feel as if you have been treated unfairly. What can you agree on, and what can you do about it? Solicit stories like that about my cousin.

Exercise for an Individual

Think of a time when you felt a sense of injustice, that life was unfair, and that people didn't understand. What can you make to deal with this feeling? Take a look at the history of almost any organization, and you will probably find that it was created out of passion inspired by a sense of injustice or unfairness. You, too, can create in this manner. Just look about you at the philanthropists in your own community and join them.

Ways Teachers can Embed the Inspiration of the Sense of Injustice as an Impetus for Creativity

Table 3.7. Ways to embed the inspiration of the sense of injustice

Ways Teachers can Embed the Inspiration of the Sense of Injustice

- Have students decide upon, through research, a social justice or community service project in your own community. Design a plan to promote its solution, or to help.
- Have students research the needs of various community service organizations and volunteer. Have them make a creative work in response to their experiences. Here are examples.[145]
- Take photos during an event about the issue and donate them to the event organizers.
- Make an exhibit about the issue.
- Set up a web page for the issue.

- Share a talent through teaching a class about the issue.
- Stage a carnival to promote spirit and knowledge about the issue.
- Produce a newspaper with articles about the issue.
- Set up an art exhibit at a local business, school or nursing home about the issue.
- Design a mural or quilt highlighting the issue.
- Form a band with your friends and give free concerts, singing songs that teach about the issue that inspires you.
- Get your marital arts or dance class to give a demonstration at a youth center, nursing home or school, emphasizing the issue that inspires you.
- Write and produce a play about the issue.
- Organize a community run or walk about the issue.

CHAPTER 3

MY THOUGHTS AND INSIGHTS ABOUT INSPIRATION
FROM A SENSE OF INJUSTICE

Possibilities:

– How does injustice inspire you?
– What does creativity have to do with social justice and injustice?
– Make an image (drawing, creative writing, music, photography, dance, diagram, skit, etc.) of inspiration from a sense of justice.

Reprise

The "I" of Inspiration does not end here; the ideas and suggestions and comments above are just a beginning. Feel free to add your own. The important point is that the creative process is enhanced by inspiration, and inspiration in creative people leads to action, to "making"—creating—something because of that inspiration.

SUMMARY OF KEY POINTS

1. Creators often find inspiration from love, desire, and the feelings engendered. This is historically called the visitation of the muse.
2. Creators are often inspired by nature.
3. Creators are often inspired by the transpersonal.
4. Creators may use substances to help with inspiration to create.
5. Creators often feel inspired from others' works, both within and across domains.
6. Creators find inspiration from dreams.
7. Creators often make creative works that were inspired from travel.
8. Creators create works after experiencing tragedy.
9. Creators feel inspired by being thwarted, and create out of a feeling for revenge or for communicating the humiliation.
10. Creators create from feeling a sense of injustice and from a need for justice.

CHAPTER 4

THE SIX OTHER I'S

The other six "I's" are discussed in this chapter. These are imagery, imagination, intuition, incubation, insight, and improvisation.

THE "I" OF IMAGERY

Imagery is also part of the creative process. The term *imagery* is psychological, the ability to mentally represent imagined or previously perceived objects accurately and vividly. Imagery is an attribute of imagination. Imagery is not only visual, but also auditory, tactile, olfactory, and gustatory. Three types of studies of creativity and imagery have been done; (1) biographical and anecdotal studies of creators telling about their personal imagery and how it inspired them; (2) studies which compared people's ability to create imagery and their scores on certain tests of creative potential; and (3) studies about creative imagery and creative productivity.[146]

Imagery is so natural to people that it almost goes without noticing. Take the creation of metaphors. Metaphors abound in human speech and writing. In fact, all metaphors are images for what is signified, helping people to see things better. A whole science of metaphor exists, which is too arcane to go into here, but the reader can notice metaphor in any magazine or television advertisement. Metaphor is the very way we see life, one may argue.

Advertising creators have great skill in this; the image of the bored Maytag repairman has been implanted in a society's psyche so that one just knows that Maytags don't need servicing very often. The image of the rough, tough, craggy man on a horse is associated with the Marlboro cigarette that hangs out of his mouth. The black and white photographs of languid anorexic European-looking teenagers with drug habits lounging around on the beach is the image of Calvin Klein for Americans who are not so slim, not so bored, and not so vacant. The image of singing fish on the wall ordering the man to give him back his filet of fish raised fish sandwich sales at McDonald's. The old lady asking where the beef was did the same at Wendy's. People watch the Super Bowl for advertising images. Babies talking about trading stocks from their high chairs and cowboys herding cats attract as many viewers as are attracted by the football.

To create an image that functions as a metaphor in words is what creative writers do. The word signifies the image and the skillful writer chooses the proper word or combinations of words to do the signifying. Read the various shades of white named in your local paint store: "pure white," "Zurich white," "rhinestone," "off white," "Navajo white," "ambience white," "city loft," "minimal white," "light moves," "white wool," "antique white," "Bauhaus buff," "nostalgia white," or "aria ivory" which do you "see" through the words chosen by the writers who named these shades? The adjectival metaphors, the nouns associated with shades of white bounce off the recognition of the reader. Which do you want on your walls? Or of green: "gallery green," "Majorca green," "acanthus," "Regina mist," "bayberry," or "billiard green"? You say you can't tell until you see the variations of shades; the written and the visual are here combined and the choice is often agonizing to the fussy decorator. The name of the shade doesn't matter, but yet it does. The evocation of image through word is here illustrated.

Examples from Creators of the "I" of Imagery

Darwin saw evolution as the image of a branching tree; Einstein pictured what it would be like to fly next to a beam of light: "If a person could run after a light wave with the same speed as light you would have a wave arrangement which could be completely independent of time."[147] Einstein learned to make visual thought experiments in his high school at Arau, which was run on the Pestalozzi theories that "Visual understanding is the essential and only true means of teaching how to judge things correctly."

Architect Maya Lin, who won the competition for the design of the Vietnam War Memorial in Washington, DC when she was still in college, deliberately tries not to create an image when she is working on an idea. That is because imagery is so powerful. She argued that creating an image immediately might lead to a sort of premature closure. She said, "In anything I've done, what I will do is resist picking up a pen, except to write, for as long as I can. And what I want to do is try to understand what I want to do as an idea."[148] She researches about the site—its history, its culture—before creating the image. "I try to think of a work as an idea without a shape. If I find the shape too soon—especially for the memorials, which have a function—then I might be predetermining a form and then stuffing the function into the form."

Guided imagery training goes on in schools, in athletics, and in business and industry. This training attempts to help people learn to manipulate images in their minds. The 2010 Winter Olympics television coverage showed skiers such as gold medal winners Lindsay Vonn and Bode Miller with eyes closed, imaging the course they were about to ski. In guided imagery a leader reads a script, with pauses, that suggests images to the people in the group, who sit in a receptive manner, quietly, with eyes closed. Imagery is essentially spatial, and as such, concrete evidence of the mind's power to construct. Coaches teach athletes to image their performances before they do them; they visualize the ski run, the football play, or the course for the marathon. Studies have shown that athletes who use imagery perform better.[149]

Exercise for a Group or for Staff Development

In creativity group, members experience an example of guided imagery.[150] Group members then think of ways they could use imagery in their own practice (see Table 3.1). One wrote, "I love the imagery exercise. It feels so real – helps create so much in my mind. It also makes me feel so calm and centered. I also like closing my eyes. Using the mind's eye is a great skill. I think we should all develop the ability to create in our heads." The group does an exercise called "Ten Minute Movie," in which group members, in groups of two or three are randomly given a time and a place, and they must create a storyboard for a movie based in that time and place.

Exercises for an Individual

- Practice creating images from thoughts. You may use similes (this is like ...) or metaphors (this is ...). Draw them or write them in your Thoughtlog.
- Mentally image a lemon. Now mentally suck it. Feel the juices in your cheeks spurt. This is gustatory imagery. Draw it or write a poem about it.
- Mentally image the smell of your favorite flower. Feel the smile in the nose. This is olfactory imagery. Draw it or sing a song about it.
- Mentally image touching the soft fur of your favorite pet or mentally stroke the cheek of your newborn baby. This is tactile imagery. Draw it or dance about it.
- Mentally image yourself winning a race in your favorite sport. Take yourself through the whole process, in all the moves. This combines visual imagery with tactile imagery. Make a flowchart.
- Mentally image the voice of your mother, father, or favorite teacher saying one of his/her famous sayings. This is auditory imagery. Imitate her.

Ways Teachers can Embed the "I" of Imagery into Their Curricula

Here are some ways that teachers can use imagery to enrich their classroom curricula. These are suggestions by teachers from the creativity groups.

Table 4.1. Ways teachers can embed the "I" of imagery

Ways Teachers can Embed the "I" of Imagery into their Classrooms

General

- Students create their own images for things they need to remember.
- Have students image themselves completing a goal or obstacle. Visualize what it would like and feel like to achieve that.
- When students are too wound up, help them find their "inner" adult by asking them to visualize themselves in the future.

Social Studies

- Imagery could be used to set the stage for an event in history. Students would close their eyes and listen as the teacher painted a word picture of the scene. Descriptions of the place, the people, the emotion, the action give a clear sense of what it was like to be there.

— Students would be given the name and description of a character they will play in a dramatic representation of the event in time. They will imagine themselves as the character and "act" accordingly.

— Before reading Susan B. Anthony's speech, "Are Women Persons," create an imagery exercise about women and men coming to hear her speak. Maybe a woman with her child in arms. Jeers in the background. Loud noise. Posters on both sides of issue. After giving a chance to imagine setting, I will read the speech.

Language Arts

— As a pre-writing exercise, they could make drawings, not using any words until the images were all released from their minds.

— Assign a writing exercise requiring students to write descriptions of images, without transitions or paragraphs, around the theme of a journey or a dream.

— Students always write better and more naturally after the teacher shows them video excerpts concerning the historical facts and commentary from the time and place that we are studying. This is partly due to them acquiring background knowledge, but more because the images in the film connect with the images in their own minds and blend to form new images in their writing.

— Use paintings and other artworks as writing prompts. Visual images transform and become written images.

— Use imagery before beginning a literary unit. With *Great Expectations*, my students close their eyes and I take them on a trip to the graveyard. Pip is alone, meets the convict.

— Poetry: Students close their eyes and listen to a poem. Have them draw or write down images.

— Discuss the importance of visualizing scenes from what you're reading to deepen understanding.

Mathematics

— Forming the semi-regular polyhedra from the regular polyhedra; imagine the truncation of the vertices – see the new faces. Use images to predict and then concretely verify those images.

Science

— Use imagery when studying bees. By using cups with different scents the students will explore how bees use their senses to find the pollen that needs to be collected. By using their sense of hearing, students will listen to the flight of the bumblebee to imagine the sounds of a busy bee hive.

– Use imagery as anticipatory set to understand different processes– water cycle, food chain, flow of electricity; history, health (Magic School Bus series).

Music

– Play evocative music and have them draw pictures while the music is playing, or tell stories about what images the music made them think of.

Art

– Setting a scene is a great way to make students think visually. Take turns describing a place while the other students draw that place.

– Students close eyes and imagine their own "happy place"–have them create the place in a picture (through art)

CHAPTER 4

MY THOUGHTS AND INSIGHTS ON THE "I" OF IMAGERY

Possibilities:

- What is the difference between imagery and imagination?
- Make an image (drawing, creative writing, music, photography, dance, diagram, skit, etc.) about the "I" of Imagery.

THE "I" OF IMAGINATION

Imagination in the creative process refers to a mental faculty whereby one can create concepts or representations of objects not immediately present or seen. Imagination is a deepening of imagery.

The topic of imagination has generated much debate and thought in the area of philosophical aesthetics. French philosopher, playwright, and novelist Jean Paul Sartre wrote a book on imagination in which he proposed that imagination is more real than actual sensory perception, and thus imagination frees us, existentially.[151] The Greek philosopher Aristotle considered works of the imagination such as poetry, drama, and fiction, more true than history because the artist could fabricate truth from the elements of history rather than exhaustively tell all the facts. The artist is able to tell the truth on a deep level, being able to see the patterns, and the overarching themes, using the imagination.

Working from the imagination is both stimulating and entertaining. Visual imagination is not the only kind that creators use. Composers imagine works in their "mind's ear," and mechanics imagine problems in their physical, spatial, array. Imaginative thought is also called daydreaming, and may be called night dreaming, as well as being called fantasy. Imagination contains known images, but also creates new images. When working from imagination, creators experience glee, a type of joy that makes one laugh, snort, and emote.

Everyone has a memory of the freedom of childhood play, of being free from the eyes and presence of adults, of running and pretending and making up stories until the summer day leads into dusk, then evening, and the adults call, ending the sweet fantasies enacted with the gang. To recapture that freedom of fantastical storytelling is the job of the "I" of Imagination.

Examples from Creators of the "I" of Imagination

Inventor Nicoli Tesla had, from his childhood, an imagination that could create images of inventions, without the help of drawings. Tesla wrote in a 1919 essay about his inventions,

> When I get an idea I start at once building it up in my imagination. I change the construction, make improvements and operate the device in my mind. It is absolutely immaterial to me whether I run my turbine in my thought or test it in my shop. I even note if it is out of balance.[152]

Russian actor and director Constantin Stanislavski has a whole chapter on imagination in his groundbreaking 1936 book, *An Actor Prepares.* He described his fictional director (his own persona, which he had to suppress because of censorship) inviting the cast to come to his apartment, where he pointed at the objects in the room, pointing out a sketch by Chekhov for the scene design of his last play. "Who would believe that this was painted by a man who, in all his life, never stirred beyond the suburbs of Moscow? He made an arctic scene out of what he saw around him at home in winter, from stories and scientific publications, from photographs. Out of all that material his imagination painted a picture."[153] He went on to give the group, over a period of weeks, exercises to develop their imaginations as actors. His method became known as The Method, and it inspired actors throughout the world, including Marlon Brando and others who studied at the Stella Adler studio. Adler was a disciple of Stanislavski's. Stanislavski emphasized sense memory, and extolled his students about imagination, thus:

Every Movement you Make on the Stage, Every Word you Speak,
is the Result of the Right Life of your Imagination.

If you speak any lines, or do anything, mechanically, without fully realizing who you are, where you came from, why what you want, where you are going, and what you will do when you get there, you will be acting without imagination.... If I ask you a perfectly simple question now, "Is it cold out today?"... you should, in your imagination, go back on to the street and remember how you walked or rode. You should test your sensations by remembering how the people you met were wrapped up ... how the snow crunched underfoot ... If you adhere strictly to this rule ... you will find your imagination developing and growing in power.[154]

Writer John Updike said that said that creative imagination "is wholly parasitic upon the real world ... Creation." This imagination is two-sided, the outer side seeks an audience and the inner side intersects with "reality itself... whatever may be true in painting or music, there is no such thing as abstract writing."

Some writers connect imagination and dreaming. Novelist John Gardner said, "Out of the artist's imagination, as out of nature's inexhaustible well, pours one thing after another. The artist composes, writes, or paints just as he dreams, seizing whatever swims close to his net. This, not the world seen directly, is his raw material." Poet Denise Levertov said, "Imagination, that breathing of life into the dust, is present in us all embryonically manifests itself in the life of dream and in that manifestation shows us the possibility: to permeate, to quicken, all of our life and the works we make." Levertov described how in a dream she went to the mirror and saw the dream character, a woman with hair wet with a spidery net of diamond-like water drops from misty fields, and said that the very detail of the woman in the mirror was evidence for the "total imagination," which is different from the intellect. She called it the "creative unconscious."

Mathematician Steven Strogratz wrote about the use of the imagination in the creation of fractals, which require the understanding of the square roots of negative numbers, which logically, don't exist as negatives because when you multiply two negatives you get a positive. "The square root of -1 still goes by the demeaning name of i, this scarlet letter serving as a constant reminder of its "imaginary" status." However, you need to continue to imagine: "But with enough imagination, our minds can make room for i as well. It lives off the number line, at right angles to it, on its own imaginary axis. And when you fuse that imaginary axis to the ordinary "real" number line, you create a 2-D space — a plane — where a new species of numbers lives." These are complex numbers, which are "the holy grail," where fractals and binary calculations begin.[155]

Exercise for a Group or for Staff Development

In creativity group, the group members rummage through a costume trunk, choose a costume, and form teams whereby they imagine a myth of creation for an animal mask. They then act out the myth. This exercise ends up in hilarity, as well as profundity, and illustrates, in a short concrete way, how the imagination, when permitted, is used in creating literary works and works of the body such as theater and dance.

Exercises for an Individual

- Join a community theater group or workshop, and, when you get a role, throw yourself into pretending. Truly suppose you are the person you are cast to be.
- Imagine you are somewhere in time, sometime in time—give yourself an age, a gender, a costume. Sit there with your eyes closed, and tell the story of this person.
- Play dolls.
- Play cowboys.
- Play war.
- Play paintball.
- Play Dungeons and Dragons or other fantasy games.
- Join a re-enactment group and re-enact their passion.
- Find a child and tell him/her a bedtime story that you make up as you go along.

Ways Teachers can Use the "I" of Imagination

The classroom is a place for hard work and, increasingly, drill, repetition, and teaching about how to get the right answers on tests. Take a break sometimes and "play."

Table 4.2. Ways teachers can use the "I" of imagination

Ways Teachers can Use the "I" of Imagination

- Create an "imagination corner" in your classroom, with appropriate prompts for the use of imagination. (Yes, secondary teachers of basic and advanced subject matter, this means you, too.)
- Have students remember incidents, tell stories, and teach them to exaggerate playfully. The delight that imagination enhances should be noted.

- Emphasize play as an initial activity for any topic. Like adults at conferences, have imaginative warm-up activities for getting acquainted, beginning a new unit, changing settings.
- Help students walk in the shoes of other students. Teach students to imagine how others think and feel and to understand that certain phrases/actions may be harmful, if not debilitating, to another student.

MY THOUGHTS AND INSIGHTS ON THE "I" OF IMAGINATION

Possibilities:

- What would the world be like without imagination?
- When you are imagining things, how do you feel?
- Make an image (drawing, creative writing, music, photography, dance, diagram, skit, etc.) of the "I" of Imagination.

THE "I" OF INTUITION

Intuition is having a hunch. "Just knowing," having a gut feeling. Again, the philosophers have discussed intuition since Plato and Aristotle, through Descartes, to Kant, to Bergson and Husserl. I won't go into this complicated esoterica, except to say that the discussion of intuition has evolved from being a discussion of a type of intellectual closure (e.g. 2 + 2 is, intuitively, 4) to a discussion that intuition is completely non-intellectual.[156] Bergson described his intuition about intuition as one of the most meaningful of his life. He was a professor of philosophy at a university in France, and it just came to him that the rational is not rational, and that the not rational is necessary. Psychologists giving certain tests and checklists have concluded that creative people trust and prefer to use their intuition.

Everyone has intuition, but many don't trust their intuition. Intuition is ambiguous, nebulous. For example, skipping steps in mathematics is an indicator that intuition is being used. Paul Erdös frustrated even fellow mathematicians with his tendency to skip steps and then expect that people understand him).[157] Those who prefer the intuitive often prefer not to read technical manuals, but jump straight to the tasks, using trial and error to solve the problems.

Intuition is not verifiable by scientific or empirical means, which leads experimentalists to say that it doesn't matter if it can't be verified to exist, and the trusters in the mysterious to say, well, of course. Intuition seems to be a personality preference on the MBTI for artists, scientists, and writers, entrepreneurs, mathematicians, actors, inventors, and composers[158]. Biographical information, testing, historical and archival research, and experimental studies have shown that creative people use intuition in doing their work.

The place of intuition in creating has long been honored. Jung thought that intuition was a message from the collective unconscious of the archetypes of the deep human experience. He defined intuition as "neither sense nor perception … a content presents itself whole and complete, without our being able to explain or discover how this content came into existence." Jung wrote about introverted intuition, that it makes mystical dreamers, creative artists, or cranks: "If he is an artist, he reveals strange, far-off things in his art, shimmering in all colours, at once portentous and banal, beautiful and grotesque, sublime and whimsical. If not an artist, he is frequently a misunderstood genius."[159] Malcolm Gladwell wrote a book called *Blink*, in which he said that people use the first 2 seconds after encountering something new to make a decision, but he was adamant in saying that this was rapid cognition, and not intuition, as intuition is too emotional:

> You could also say that it's a book about intuition, except that I don't like that word. In fact it never appears in "Blink." Intuition strikes me as a concept we use to describe emotional reactions, gut feelings–thoughts and impressions that don't seem entirely rational.[160]

Now who's splitting hairs, Mr. Gladwell? says this reader.

Daniel Cappon made a helpful list of the skills that are inquired for intuition. They consist of the basic skills and the higher skills, and are arranged in a hierarchy from lower to higher.[161]

1. Utilizing quick eyes (recognizing an object exposed for 1/25 seconds).
2. Seeing through things (recognizing an object through a whiteout).
3. Finding things in a crowd (needle in the haystack or "Where's Waldo?" (the kids' game).
4. Recognizing similar objects from successive exposures.
5. Recognizing dissimilar objects from successive exposures
6. Putting things together (assembling a jigsaw puzzle).
7. Estimating present time flow.
8. Employing quick memory (instant recall of different objects in a crowded space).
9. Knowing what one didn't know one knew (puzzling out a word or symbol from a foreign language, or naming an object and its use from the very ancient past).
10. Using spontaneous imagery such as imagining things on a plain wall.
11. Associative imagery related to a picture (active imagination).
12. Knowledge of what will happen next (anticipation or foresight, such as predicting what will happen next in an evolving event, as when a goalie knows where to be in order to save a goal).
13. Best timing (knowing exactly when to take the right step or action).
14. The hunch (perception of a problem's ultimate optimal solution, such as the foot-of-bed medical diagnosis).
15. The best way (choice of optimal method, e.g., knowing what steps to take in order to solve a problem).
16. The best application of a discovery (optimal future application of a discovery, such as foreseeing aerodynamic transportation from flying a kite).
17. Hindsight (perceiving the causality or aetiology of a medical problem or discovering the steps of a process).
18. Associative matching (assortative cognitive synthesis, such as matching a child's face to his or her face as an adult).
19. Dissociative matching (dissortative cognitive synthesis, e.g., being able to tell who didn't belong in a group picture of a family with one stranger in it).
20. The meaning of things (teleological ideation, such as understanding the meaning of archetypes, symbols, religious rituals, etc., or the meaning of an event).

As a possible illustration, with regard to number 20, visual artist Stuart Davis said, "What I'm trying to do is resolve my daily intuitive questions into a practical visual logic that will last through the night. And if it lasts through the night it will last forever."[162]

Of course, we must not forget that teaching itself is an intuitive practice, despite the attempts of overseers to make it concrete and accountable. The teacher constantly intuits, thinks on her feet, understands instantly what the student is driving at, and what is the best way to respond. Teaching is improvising and reacting in the instant. The more one teaches, the more intuitive one is; a deep knowledge of the techniques of pedagogical interaction is embedded into the teacher's repertoire by the time she has been teaching for awhile. No lesson plans for how to teach will suffice; teaching well also needs gut reactions and intuition. Christopher Bache, a college professor, has written a book about how intuition feeds upon synchronicity while the teaching is going on. He called it "a mysterious interweaving of minds," and "the magic." [163]

> When the magic happened, the walls of our separate minds seemed to come down temporarily, secrets were exchanged, and healing flowed. When the magic happened, my students and I tapped into levels of creativity beyond our separate capacities … If I cut myself off from my intuition … I would also be cutting myself off from a creativity that was benefiting my teaching in very tangible ways.

Exercise for a Group or for Staff Development

The importance of intuitive perception of the world, of a non-concrete but still tangible apprehension of underlying truth informs the creator's view of life. Instruct the group to sit back to back, and try to send a message, one at a time, to the person behind them. They then give each other feedback. It is sometimes amazing what people are able to intuit. Others get nothing, but still remember that intuition is mysterious and ephemeral.

Another exercise is Zen sketching. [164] Project a series of art works on the screen in a darkened room, and have group members quickly sketch the outlines. This helps them see the big picture, a characteristic of the intuitive perceiver. This also can be used to illustrate insight, as they immediately see the negative and positive space in the illustrations.

One teacher said, about intuition:

Intuition is something that children recognize. They already know it and are comfortable with whatever it is that they know. Therefore, they should be allowed to explore it fully. Intuition will be the base, and from it will extend elaboration and the development of their gifts.

Exercises for the Individual

- Try some of the types of intuition that Cappon (see above) has categorized
- Play games that require intuition such as Battleship, bridge, or Clue.
- Do jigsaw puzzles.
- Guess. Pay attention to your hunches.

The suppression and disparaging of intuition by the rational is rife; try to treasure your intuition and practice using it.

Ways Teachers can Embed the "I" of Intuition into the Classroom

Again, the classroom is supposed to be a place of logic, of judgment, of order and predictability, but experienced teachers "just know" things about procedures, students, and colleagues. "Is anything wrong?" one says to another as they stand by the mailboxes, before they even speak. "What's going on?" says the principal, as she stands at the doorway welcoming students, and suspects a supposedly innocent gang of being up to something. Management by Walking Around, a famous strategy for administrators and teachers, relies on the experienced educators' intuition to divine what's up. Here is a table (Table 3.3) of some ways to honor intuition that teachers have recommended.

Table 4.3. Ways teachers can embed the "I" of intuition

Ways Teachers can Embed the "I" of Intuition into their Classrooms

General Classroom

- Have a discussion of intuition–has it affected them in any way? and then have students generate examples to spur an awareness.
- Have students make predictions about the rest of the day (phrases they may hear, what they expect for dinner, etc.) Then they can watch and listen. This might heighten awareness of what is going on around them.
- Discuss safety issues. Define, discuss, share–safe situation vs. unsafe. If your gut tells you it's wrong, it is wrong. Help young children recognize and appreciate their "gut reactions"; "feelings" about situations in their lives from an early age. The safety message of if it feels wrong or bad, it probably is. Run!
- Recognize hunches and relate it to the hunches described by creators—inventors, athletes, scientists, mathematicians.
- Discuss testing strategies–often the first answer one thinks of is the right one.
- Talk about times they followed/didn't follow their intuition. What can we learn from this? Expose them to intuition as a part of them-selves; they may not realize it.
- Look for examples of characters in books using intuition.
- Many kids are very intuitive and it is almost like a breakthrough for them when they realize others have it too. Just ask, "What is intuition?" The question generates discussion and deep thought.
- Honor children's choices about what they think they should do with their lives.
- Let kids explore times they "just know." Allow a correct outcome w/out requiring the steps to it. Talk, journal about places that make kids feel good/bad. Trust the kids. Allow alternative explanations. Be open to interpretations based on feelings. Don't overthink.

- Working with intuition with the kids could include work with the invention process. If they go with their "gut instinct" rather than try to "overthink" everything, what will solve this problem? How will it work?

Mathematics

- Play some strategy games/ideas where they can try to figure out what someone else will do before they make their move – analysis.
- Play Battleship
- Interdisciplinary Arts and history
- Study a painting before reading about a period of history and ask them to use their intuition to read the artist's message before. Use a representative piece of music in the background as the piece.

Language Arts

- Read science fiction/fantasy writing. The characters often operate on intuition. Have them recognize when and how it works.
- Write a story without an outline, intuitively creating a plot.

MY THOUGHTS AND INSIGHTS ON THE "I" OF INTUITION

Possibilities:

– Describe a time when you had a hunch and it paid off.
– What does Davis mean when he says "If it lasts through the night it will last forever"?
– Make an image (drawing, creative writing, music, photography, dance, diagram, skit, etc.) of intuition.

THE "I" OF INCUBATION

Incubation as a part of the creative process occurs when the mind is at rest. The body is at rest. The creator has gone on to something else. The problem is percolating silently through the mind and body. But somewhere, inside, down there below the surface, the dormant problem is arising. A solution is sifting. Incubation was one of the steps in Wallas' four-part description of problem solving.[165]

Psychologists speak of an "incubation effect," which may be caused by conscious work on the problem, and after wards, overwhelming fatigue, where what doesn't work has been forgotten.[166] While resting, the mind works on putting unlike things together. All the ideas may be assimilated through this time period. Then awareness comes and the answer is there.

Experiments have shown that if people are given a problem and told to solve it right away, they solve it less successfully than if they are given the problem and told to go away and think about it. The psychological research on incubation often uses insight problems where the problem solvers reach an impasse and must take a break before coming upon the answers to the problems.[167] Some evidence also exists that using forced incubation, that is, intentionally putting aside a creative project and letting it bake, so to speak, results in more creative products.[168]

Examples from Creators of the "I" of Incubation

People often incubate while driving, sleeping, exercising, even showering. Kary Mullis, a Nobel-prize winner, came up with PCR (Polymerase chain reaction) while driving.[169] Novelist Gabriel Garcia Marquez, while he was a reporter was driving one day between Acapulco and Mexico City. He perceived the first chapter of *One Hundred Years of Solitude*. He went home, told his wife not to disturb him, and for the next 18 months, he closed himself into a room for up to ten hours a day, and wrote the novel.[170] Child developmental psychologist Jean Piaget said: "When I have done a number of chapters I leave them for six months in a drawer, to reread later. One then senses what is missing, what must be developed or shortened."[171]

Exercise for a Group or for Staff Development

In creativity group, incubation is illustrated by the individual creativity project, which is the final product. Group members spend days (some who prefer Judging and Sensing on the MBTI know instantly what they will do, but others take time), weeks, and months thinking of what they will do for this project. "Let it incubate," the leader should say. "You'll know what you will do when you know what you will do." The leader must approve this project, and have ongoing discussions with the group members, as they incubate about it. Then, when they choose their products, they incubate about how to present it, and how to make it.

Exercise for an Individual

Put it away. Stop work on it just as you are revving up. Go and do something else. Sleep on it. Pay attention to your thoughts and even your dreams throughout the days, weeks, months, year. Let it rest. You are incubating and the insight will come.

Ways Teachers can Embed the "I" of Incubation Into the Classroom

The natural way to do this is to give a specific time period for assignments before they are due. Make it conscious, though. The literature on metacognition suggests that reminders and a schedule for certain aspects of the assignment to be completed along a timeline helps students get things made.

Table 4.4. Ways teachers can embed the "I" of incubation

Ways Teachers can Embed the "I" of Incubation

– Subscribe to the project curriculum orientation. The recent emphasis on 21st Century Skills emphasizes collaboration and projects. Give group and individual projects, with a timeframe that gives enough time for thought. Set a time when students must tell you what their project will entail, but don't demand specific steps or details, as these will change as they incubate. Ask for progress reports so they will have the self-discipline to complete the project.

– Use technology for collaboration with distant partners. Several ongoing quest systems exist, such as ThinkQuest, where students collaborate with students in a different place, country, location. Emphasize that the projects need downtime, where one can think and plan and come up with variations, methods, and new ways.

CHAPTER 4

MY THOUGHTS AND INSIGHTS ON THE "I" OF INCUBATION

Possibilities:

– Describe a time when you incubated a creative solution.
– How does incubation work in the mind and body?
– Make an image (drawing, creative writing, music, photography, dance, diagram, skit, etc.) about incubation.

THE "I" OF INSIGHT

Insight in the creative process is the ability to see and understand clearly the inner nature of things, especially by intuition. Cognitive psychologists have researched several types of insight. The studies have shown that insight has the appearance of suddenness, requires preparatory hard work, relies on reconceptualization, involves old and new information; and applies to ill-structured problems.

Insight involves restructuring the problem so that it can be seen in a different way. Many notable creative works have originated from insights. When insight happens, we just have to say "Aha! So that's how it works. So that's the answer. So that's what it's all about. So that's what the pattern is." The most famous image of insight is that of Archimedes rising from the bathtub, saying "Aha!" and running down the street, after he discovered the principle of the displacement of water. The "Aha!" comes after knowing the field really well, and after incubation. However, the insights are often a series of small progressive insights as the creator thinks about the problem or creation.[172]

Examples from Creators of the "I" of Insight

Physicist J. Robert Oppenheimer was known as an idea man. He would have the insight and publish a small paper, just ahead of the scientists who would develop the elegant solutions to the problems. He published about black holes before anyone, but then moved on to another insight and another, having no patience for developing the problem further.[173]

Steve Jobs and Steve Wozniak, who founded Apple Computers together, when they went to their first computer show, in the 1970s, saw how other companies advertised their wares and had an insight. Marketing is key. For the next computer show, they rented the first spot, near the door, and made a splashy display utilizing awe-inspiring graphics and design, even though they had not yet invented the computer. They sold out before the computer was made.

Exercise for a Group or an Individual

Zen sketching, as mentioned above, in the intuition session, also works here, to illustrate insight. Turn out the lights. Show slides of scenes. Group members must keep their eyes on the screen and quickly draw the slides. This forces insight into the layout of the slide, quick perception of what it consists of.

Group members also record their creative process of insight in their Thoughtlogs, as they decide upon their individual or group creativity projects. They cite their dreams, their walks, their drives, and such, as the moments when it all came together—their "aha!" experiences that came incrementally or all at once (big "aha" or little "ahas").

Ways Teachers can Embed the "I" of Insight

Again, making it conscious is the task. All people experience insights; the teacher's job is to help students recognize the insights.

Table 4.5. Ways teachers can embed the "I" of insight

Ways Teachers can Embed the "I" of Insight

- Intentionally define insight and talk about it, and then discuss it with the students, to have them realize its presence when they are thinking about things.
- Keep a list of students' insights and post it.
- Study the insight method of teaching math. Give students a problem without a solution. Do not teach them a model or a theorem. They will have to develop insights in order to create a mental model in order to solve or partially solve the problem. http://teachingmath. nfo/index.htm
- In language arts/literature, encourage students to write their thoughts in the text (alternatively, use sticky notes) as they have insights about the topic, the style, the thoughts. This will create a permanent record of their thoughts and will give them insight when they come back to the text. (See example of the "thoughts and insights" pages in this text.)
- Talk about your own insights.

MY THOUGHTS ON THE "I" OF INSIGHT

Possibilities:

– Describe the physical and mental circumstances of your last insight. What was it about?
– What does insight have to do with creativity?
– Make an image ((drawing, creative writing, music, photography, dance, diagram, skit, etc.) having to do with the "I" of Insight.

THE "I" OF IMPROVISATION

The importance of improvisation in the creative process cannot be understated. Improvisation is to go where you have not been before, to fly by the seat of your pants, to play it by ear, to trudge through the desert without a camel. For example, to play your musical instrument without music in front of you is frightening to some who have learned to trust in their reading ability and not in their intuition and musical memory. The idea of "play" in improvisation is a necessity. Think of children making up the game as they go along, lost in imagination, forming teams and sides in a fluid all-day motion generated by the discourse of the moment.

Examples from Creators of the "I" of Improvisation

Improvisation seems to be a key part of the creative process. Although improvisation is a key skill in the domains of music, dance, and theater, other creators also use it. Visual artist Edward Hopper relied on improvisation as he painted: "More of me comes out when I improvise."[174] The poet James Merrill used automatic writing as an improvisational technique: so did William Butler Yeats. In automatic writing you keep your pen on the paper and do not take it off and just write and write whatever comes out, without judgment.

Improvisation underlies all creativity, but in music, dance, and theater, the improvisational performer cannot revise the work as writers or painters can. Improvisation in theater and music is almost always collaborative, and requires instant communication between people in the improvisation group. The Russian composer Dmitri Shostakovich was forced to take several jobs accompanying films at the silent cinemas. During one film, called *Swamp and Water Birds of Sweden*, he improvised birds calling and singing and flying, and he was surprised when the audience began to cat call and clap. They didn't like his improvisation, but he was glad he was able to divert them from the film with his talent for doing so.[175] Later, he composed many scores for films.

Dance choreographers rely almost universally on improvisation in order to begin to make a dance. Martha Graham would begin to dance, outlining the pattern she wanted, and her dancers would imitate her. Then she would work on fixing the gestures so that the dancers would be moving together. Merce Cunningham would improvise with figures on his famous computer program for choreography. Choreographer and dancer Twyla Tharp, winner of the Kennedy Medal, called improvisation "futzing." To call it improvisation seemed too institutional. Improvisation is messy." She is

> in a certain state where the cerebral powers are turned off, and the body just goes according to directive that I know not of, it's at those times that I feel a very special connection to … I feel the most right. I don't want to become too mystic about this, but things feel as though they're in the best order at that

particular moment. It's a short period. It goes only, at maximum, an hour. But it is, that hour that ... that tells me who I am ... There are moments where things come, and they don't know where they've come from.[176]

Exercise for a Group or for Staff Development

Here are some areas in which one can improvise.

–Jazz

Play a jazz composition based on a familiar melody, a common children's song, the simpler the better. "Row row row your boat" is fine. Improvise on the melody. Afterwards, talk about the feeling of going beyond the written notes.

–Theater

Many theater games exist. Here's one. Get two volunteers for an improvisational theater exercise. One is the desk clerk and one is the person who wants a room. Conduct a conversation where each person can only ask questions. Switch. Conduct a conversation where each person can only make statements. Switch. Conduct a conversation where one person can only ask questions and the other person can only make statements. The work of Augusto Boal combines theater improvisational games and exercises with social justice themes, and is very powerful.[177] I have participated in some of these workshops, which were deeply affecting. Along the same lines, but without the social message, the work of Viola Spolin is the classic theater improvisation guide.[178] Laughter abounds. Creativity is at home with improvisational theater.

–Word Rivers and Writing Practice

Put your pen to paper and do not take it up. Write whatever comes to your mind for the next ten minutes. Begin with "I have this pen in my hand ...."

–Creative Movement

Play some music that is free form. Form a circle. Listen to the music and begin moving your arms in response. Now add your legs. Add your body. Try the floor, the mid-level position, the high-level position. Have fun. No one is watching you. In creative movement, no step is wrong; it is not rigid and one doesn't need to be able to count or imitate.

–Rhythm & Drumming

Gather a series of items that can make noise; pots, pans, sticks, tubs, bells, whistles, and the like. Play a video of the group "Stomp" or of a drumming group to demonstrate briefly. Divide into small groups. Create a musical piece that utilizes rhythm and drumming. Present it to the group.

—Scat Singing

Play a recording of Ella Fitzgerald or Mel Tormé scat singing. Scat singing is improvisation with the voice. The singer uses nonsense syllables and moves along with the accompaniment, becoming, virtually, one of the musical instruments. Now, as a group, sing along with them. Doobie doobie do.[179]

–Doodling

Read the group a story. They must doodle while they are listening. Tell them about how President Kennedy's doodles during important security meetings sold for big sums of money. While doodling, breathe deeply, and listen and let what comes out come out. This can also be done while listening to music.

–Joke-telling

Lighten up. Humor is a definite part of the creative process. Developmental and cultural, humor is so idiosyncratic that at different ages and in different lands, we laugh at different jokes, though slapstick humor seems to be universal. Improvise by joke telling. Sit around and tell funny stories—clean, of course! After everyone has told a joke, talk about the effect on the group feeling. Joke telling and humor increase the confidence for the core attitude of risk-taking.

–Story-telling

Someone begins by telling a story, perhaps an apocryphal family story about a relative, the one that everyone tells when they get together. The story will remind someone of another story, and that person will jump in, telling that story. That story will remind someone else of a story, and that person will tell that story. Proceed until everyone has a chance to tell a story. There is no set order of participation, and people can tell more than one story, but no one should dominate.

–Dance

Dance is also improvisational, if one goes to a club or a special event. In group, you can dance to a video by dancer Gabrielle Roth, who is a teacher of dance as creative and spiritual practice. Students improvise on several rhythms: largo, staccato, etc., are demonstrated and the group members follow.[180]

Ways Teachers can Embed the "I" of Improvisation

See above. Many good books on improvisation exist. Among them is Bernardi's *Improvisation Starters and Newton's improvisation book.*

MY THOUGHTS AND INSIGHTS ON THE "I" OF IMPROVISATION

Possibilities:

– List and reflect on some times when you improvised.
– How difficult is improvisation?
– Improvise an image (drawing, creative writing, music, photography, dance, diagram, skit, etc.).

CHAPTER 4

Are there SEVEN "I's"?

The Seven I's are, of course, somewhat arbitrarily chosen, based on the stories of creators about their creative process, but made into a list by me. All creators do not use all the I's, but most use most. A friend has suggested adding the "I" of Intent. Another friend has suggested that the I of Imagery and the I of Imagination are too similar. The point is that there is a psychological research literature on each of them, and that they are a main aspect of the creative process, and that you can incorporate them into your own creativity, whether there are 8 "I's" or 6.

SUMMARY OF KEY POINTS

1 The "I" of Imagery can be visual, auditory, gustatory, tactile, or olfactory.
2 The "I" of Imagination contains imagery but is related to the process of play, fantasy, and story.
3 The "I" of Intuition is basic and consists of gut feeling, or "just knowing."
4 The "I" of Insight values the quick "aha" that leads to creative exploration.
5 The "I" of Incubation signals a slow down and wait trust that the insight is coming.
6 The "I" of Improvisation is aligned to the idea of play.

CHAPTER 5

GENERAL PRACTICES IN THE CREATIVE PROCESS

In the studies, biographies, and memoirs of, by, and about real creators that form the research base of this book, several other aspects of the creative process seem apparent: (1) the need for solitude; (2) creativity rituals; (3) meditation; (4) exercise, especially walking; (5) the quest for silence; (6) divergent production practice; and (7) creativity as the process of a life.

THE NEED FOR SOLITUDE

Often, a crucial part of the creative process in domains such as creative writing, music composition, mathematics, and visual arts, is solitude. Solitude is not loneliness, but a fertile state where the creator can think and work freely. Psychologist Anthony Storr wrote a whole book justifying the incidence of solitude in creatives.[181] Poet Amy Clampitt said, "I think the happiest times in my childhood were spent in solitude—reading … Socially, I was a misfit."[182] Today, those who seek solitude are often looked at with pity, for people are supposed to be in society, to do social networking, to let near strangers whom they have "friended" where they are at all times via Facebook and Tweets, and to crave companionship. The Internet abounds with dating sites, comradeship sites, chat rooms, gaming sites, where for a minimal sum, people can connect with each other.

People who don't have live-in or close human relationships, who are not married, or in love, or in a family, are viewed as somehow sick. For creators, their work is often the most important thing. The iPpod may be playing, for the need for broadcast noise seems to be omnipresent, but the work is often done while in solitude. Creative people may be solitary, but that doesn't make them neurotic or unhappy. Some even say that there is something transcendental about solitude. When the person is suddenly alone and able to concentrate, she is able to decipher what may have seemed too puzzling, and to unite ideas that may have seemed too different. Not being able to achieve solitude frustrates many creative people. Loneliness may ensue after the solitude of working; it is then that the creator probably seeks society.

Solitude induces reverie, a state between sleeping and waking, a state of fertile relaxation, allowing images and ideas to come so that attention can be paid. What is important is a state of passivity and receptivity. Some people achieve this while cooking, cleaning, or sewing alone, walking in the woods, or during a long, boring drive.

Examples from Creators of the Need for Solitude

It is in solitude that, as theologian Martin Buber, said, "We listen to our inmost selves— and do not know which sea we hear murmuring."[183] Composer John Harbison said,

I tend to need to be by myself more. I don't know why that is, but it's true, and I tend to feel that even though I may not have a methodology, there is a solitude that is helpful to me to reinforce an inspiration. I can function, for instance, with a very small library, one that I choose, of music and books. Usually a physical environment is very helpful if there is some place to get out and walk, and if it is not horribly ugly.[184]

Poet Gary Snyder said of his call to be a poet:

As a poet, I hold the most archaic values on earth. They go back to the late Paleolithic: the fertility of the soil, the magic of animals, the power vision in solitude, the terrifying initiation and rebirth; the love and ecstasy of the dance, the common work of the tribe.

One pictures science laboratories as places of social intercourse, as teams of bright men and women work with apparatus, test tubes, computers, and calculations, freely and regularly consulting with each other. However, for Nobel Prize winner Louis Pasteur, this was emphatically not true. He was a solitary, introverted researcher. His assistants sat in small rooms or in the corners of the laboratory, working silently. They never disturbed Pasteur, except when he initiated the interaction or asked them a question. He could only think when things were silent. Once, while visiting the laboratory of one of his friends, he commented on the active scientists working together. "How can you work in the midst of such agitation?" The other scientist said that his ideas became more exciting in such a setting. Pasteur said, "It would put mine to flight."[185]

Exercise for a Group or for Staff Development

Simulate solitude. Take a full day Meditation Day field trip with the creativity group. Visit a nature spot, a museum, a cemetery, a cathedral. Practice the exercises with the Thoughtlogs as companions. During each visit (woods, cemetery, museum, cathedral or church), group members must do the activity alone, reflecting upon themselves and their thoughts. They are not permitted to speak to their group mates and as they pass each other they should just nod silently. After each time (about an hour in each place), gather at an appointed place, stand or sit in a circle, and share. Evaluations have said, "I am such a busy person; mother, teacher, student; this day gave me a chance to reflect within, in solitude. I am grateful." Others said, "The Thoughtlogs made me realize what a creative person I really am; as I made my marks each day for 10 minutes, the alone time really made me focus. I thought about things I hadn't thought about for years."

Exercise for an Individual

Go alone. When you're alone, it's just more intense.

MY THOUGHTS AND INSIGHTS ON SOLITUDE FOR CREATIVITY

Possibilities:

- Describe the last time you had solitude. How did you feel?
- Why is solitude necessary for some creators?
- Make an image (drawing, creative writing, music, photography, dance, diagram, skit, etc.) having to do with solitude for creativity.

CREATIVITY RITUALS

Ritual is any customary ceremony or observance; it is a repeated practice performed before or during creating. Ritual involves special places, special procedures, and special repetitive acts. Often associated with religions or secret societies such as fraternities, rituals are also both more mundane and more universal. Rituals can be performed by the group or by the individual. This creativity practice concerns rituals for both creative groups and creative individuals.

Examples from Creators of the Use of Ritual

Rituals practiced by creators are quite personal. The artist Arshile Gorky would, every week, scrub the parquet floor of his studio with lye, keep his hallway dark so he could see who was knocking without being observed. His biographer, said, "His working day was governed by ritual. A certain state of dreamy exhaustion was necessary, he used to say, to create freely and spontaneously."[186] Visual artist Marlene Ekola described her morning ritual as she enters her studio:

> I begin with a walking meditation around a sacred circle, with a single candle within a mound of stones. I bow. I step into the circle. I light the candle. I come out of the circle. I bow again. I walk the circle over and over and reverse the direction until I feel I've gone down deeply enough into myself to go into the work. The candle is the symbol. I am shoveling stars. I am flying birds. My life as an artist is an exploration of the deep unknown.[187]

Ritual serves to remove the creator from the outer world and propel her to the inner world. Nobel prize-winning novelist Toni Morrison enters the inner world before dawn:

> I always get up and make a cup of coffee while it is still dark … and watch the light come…. for me this ritual comprises my preparation to enter a space that I can only call nonsecular. Writers all devise ways to approach that place where they expect to make the contact, where they become the conduit, or where they engage in this mysterious process. For me, light is the signal in the transition. It's not being in the light; it's being there before it arrives.[188]

Some people walk or exercise before creating, when they often get their best ideas. Some people go for a long drive. Some arrange their rooms or desks a certain way. Some like to work at a certain time of day. The approach to the work itself is ritualistic, and the work itself could be called, perhaps, the ceremony. Rituals are individually prescribed and performed. No one can impose a ritual upon another that will be sure to prepare the creator to create. Dancer Katricia Eaglin described her pre-performance rituals. She tries to find a secluded place to think about what is coming. This may be a nearby park, but may also be the theater bathroom. On tour, before the performance, she focuses in the hotel, while absent-mindedly organizing makeup and clothes. She likes to read the chapter about noise in a favorite book, which talks about how dancers can subvert their efforts with negativity rather than preparing themselves for the performance ahead.[189]

After the morning walk, the morning work, for Russian novelist Leo Tolstoy:

I always write in the morning. I was pleased to hear lately that Rousseau too, after he got up in the morning, went for a short walk and sat down to work. In the morning one's head is particularly fresh. The best thoughts most often come in the morning after walking, while still in bed or during the walk. Many writers work at night. Dostoevesky always wrote at night. In a writer there must always be two people – the writer and the critic. And, if one works at night, with a cigarette in one's mouth, although the work of creation goes on briskly, the critic is for the most part in abeyance, and this is very dangerous.[190]

Exercise for a Group or for Staff Development

The group leader begins each session ceremonially. For example, before each group meeting, the leader asks for silence, and then, in an attunement exercise, the leader asks people to come to group, to leave the rush hour traffic behind, the thoughts and worries of the work day behind, the family concerns behind. "Come to group, come to group." In creativity group, group members are encouraged to write in their Thoughtlogs about their own rituals. They also speak of instilling certain rituals in their classrooms; for example, having everyone clean their desks before they do an activity; or having everyone breathe silently with eyes closed before writing.

Exercise for an Individual

Create your own ritual. Do the ritual before you do the work. Have a space where you do the work. Protect the ritual and the space. This is harder than you think it might be, especially if you live with a family or in a very small space. In some homes, the garage and the basement are often fitted out for hobbyists. The spare room becomes the sewing room when the nest begins to empty. My recently retired lawyer friend rented an office just across the street from her apartment, where she goes to write. She wants to write plays, and begins her daily ritual by pouring her morning coffee into a mug, locking her door, taking the elevator to the ground, crossing the street, unlocking the door, entering her office sitting at the desk, turning on her computer, and beginning. She has continued the habit of "going to work."

Ways Teachers can Embed the General Practice of Ritual Into the Classroom

Teachers in education and classroom management classes are taught to create their own classroom rituals so that the students feel safe and at home in their school-rooms and classes, and so this is not a new idea.

Table 5.1. Ways teachers can use ritual

**Ways Teachers can Use the General Practice
of Ritual in the Classroom**

– Create your own classroom rituals for beginning the day, changing activities, going out of the room, ending the day, etc. These give comfort to both you and the students and lets them know they are in a *temenos*, a sanctuary space, a classroom, where learning is valued and promised. In my own classroom(s), which are in generic college classrooms, and varied places, I begin with a gathering exercise ("Come to class now; leave the cares of your personal world behind and come to our world, here.") and ending exercise (I bow, begin applause, and say, "Thank you for a good class. We couldn't have a good class if you weren't here.")

MY THOUGHTS AND INSIGHTS ON THE GENERAL CREATIVITY PRACTICE OF RITUAL

Possibilities:

- What rituals do you practice before or during the times you are creating?
- Describe the rituals you have observed others performing during ceremonial events.
- Make an image (drawing, creative writing, music, photography, dance, diagram, skit, etc.) of an idea in this section of the chapter.

MEDITATION

Meditation is a part of the creative process in all domains. Whether or not it is formal, tied to a religion like Buddhism, or informal, tied to a need for inner quiet, creators seem to meditate. The term *meditate is* not used in the religious sense, here, but in a spiritual, individual sense.

Examples of Meditation and the Creative Process from Creators

Visual artist Morris Graves said of painting, "The act is a meditation in itself." Likewise, artist Naum Gabo said, "Art is not just pleasure; it is a creative activity of human consciousness from which all spiritual creation derives. Art is everything. Everything we make or even think about is art." [191] An anthology of poetry contained works by contemporary poets who practice Buddhism.[192] Poet Gary Snyder stated:

> In this world of onrushing events the act of meditation—even just a "one-breath" meditation—straightening the back, clearing the mind for a moment—is a refreshing island in the stream … it is a simple and plain activity. Attention; deliberate stillness and silence … the quieted mind has many paths, most of them tedious and ordinary. Then, right in the midst of meditation, totally unexpected images or feelings may suddenly erupt, and there is a way into a vivid transparency.

The vehicles for discovering one's self are breathing, sitting still, and waiting. Often the creative work follows the meditation, and the meditation is a preparatory ritual for the creative work. Singer songwriter Leonard Cohen spent years in a Buddhist monastery, and his songs bespeak the meditative creativity he has been led to share. Others have embraced the contemplative life of the Christian monastery, for example, the poets Kathleen Norris and Daniel Berrigan.

Photographer John Daido Loori described his creative journey, the workshops and retreats he has led, and the teaching he has done at Naropa University, a Zen Buddhist institution. His assertion, contrary to Gary Snyder's, is that the meditative enhances the creative process not by providing the creator with images or ideas, but by emptying and clearing the mind so that the process can happen spontaneously. He said,

> The doorway to this experience is the creative process. Please delve deeply into it. Give it a chance to do what it is capable of doing. Engage it fully with the whole body and mind. If you do, sooner or later, this limitless way of being will be your own. It will never make sense, and you'll never be able to explain it to anybody, but you still experience it, and by so doing you will make it real.[193]

Engage. Delve. Limitless. Never making sense. What "unscientific" words these are! What language used by those who treasure precision in language. In more prosaic terms, the experimental research psychologists have categorized such responses and examples as the "mystical" approach.[194] To illustrate how meditation is used, take the story told by poet Elizabeth Alexander, who was the poet at Barack Obama's inauguration, about how she composes. She keeps paper and pencil with her at all times, and goes about her daily work, picking up her children, teaching, shopping. During the day, during "meditative moments," phrases come to her. She said, "You're humble before the muse. You hope she will help. There are many false starts." Then, when she has an extended meditative time, she gathers the phrases together, writing in longhand on a legal pad, and then entering the draft into her computer, where she works and works. The meditative moments arrive with regularity, because she trusts that they will, and is prepared.[195]

Dancers have spoken of using meditation as well. Meredith Monk, Sita Mani, and Katricia Eaglin discussed how meditation helped their creative work. Monk found that meditation helped her to be kinder and more tolerant of her fellow dancers. Mani said that meditation "opens up a channel for creativity to come out." Eaglin uses meditative prayer to reflect on training classes and what she has learned.[196]

Exercise for a Group or for Staff Development

In creativity group, closed eyes, attentive posture, and deep breathing also often precede the exercises mentioned here. The Meditation Day field trip is another way in which meditation is honored.

Exercise for an Individual

Explore various meditative practices. If the accounts are to be believed, meditation attracts creative people. Do a retreat weekend at one of the many retreat sites throughout the nation and the world. Practice the breathing exercises they suggest. Your concentration and power will increase, as well as your creative thought processes. I have spent quite a few weekends at the Omega Institute north of New York City, and have enjoyed every one; I sang with the Western Wind Ensemble, with Odetta and with Bobby McFerrin and meditated with Joseph Chilton Pearce, walked the labyrinth with Lauren Artress, did the raisin meditation with Tara Bennett Goleman at a workshop on emotional intelligence, and danced with Gabrielle Roth, among others. I've also attended workshops at the Open Center and at the Pacifica Institute, including one with clergyman Ira Progoff, the inventor of process meditation, where I bought the book, which, sadly, I am still unable to read and process, it is so dense and so prescriptive.

Creativity professor and educational psychologist Diane Montgomery has meditation retreat weekends in her lake house for her students and former students who are now friends. There is an organization on meditative practice and how to embed it into the collegiate curriculum, called the Association for Contemplative Mind in Higher Education,, a division of the Center for Contemplative Mind in Society, which has regular retreats and webinars for professors and others interested, in order to "support pioneering instructors who are discovering ways to integrate contemplative practices into their teaching methods to create a deep, enriching, and transformative learning environment."[197]

Ways Teachers can Embed the Practice of Meditation into the Classroom

Meditation is paying attention in a quiet way. Gates said,

> It is the sitting meditation that Westerners most often think of as meditation. There are many forms of meditation however, including breathing, sitting, walking, yoga, loving-kindness, insight, and so forth. Indeed, meditation can be done with any activity. Hearing the telephone ring, stopping at a red light, washing dishes, drinking tea, and eating a tangerine identify a few of the day-to-day kinds of activities that can be easily used for meditation.[198] Researchers are beginning to find that meditative practices help with the atmosphere in the classroom.

Table 5.2. Meditation

Ways Teachers can Embed the General Creativity Practice of Meditation in Their Classrooms
– Pause. Breathe. Don't rush. Begin activities with closed eyes and a deep breath.
– Have students "put on their game face" before performances or practices by encouraging them to close their eyes, sit still, breathe, and visualize themselves.
– Talk about and research the classroom use of meditation.[199]
– Use bells or a bronze begging bowl with a mallet to signal a period of quiet and mindfulness in the classroom. The very sounds of these musical instruments seems to induce a creative frame of mind.
– Emphasize slowness rather than quickness. Berkman (1995), in speaking of mathematics, said, that math teachers should model "mathematical behavior to show that understanding comes from effort and meditation, not from the snappy phenomenon known as 'getting it.'"[200]

MY THOUGHTS AND INSIGHTS ON THE CREATIVITY PRACTICE OF MEDITATION

Possibilities:

- What is your experience with meditation?
- Why would meditation enhance the creative process?
- Make an image (drawing, creative writing, music, photography, dance, diagram, skit, etc.) on some idea in this section.

EXERCISE, ESPECIALLY WALKING

One could call exercise a ritual, but I am going to treat it separately here, because it is so pervasive in the biographical material. It is fascinating to reflect on the importance of walking in the creative process.

Examples from Creators of the Importance of Exercise for the Creative Process

Up until the 20th century, certain European males went on what was called the year of wandering, the *Wanderschafte*, whereby the young men would seek to find themselves. Psychologist Erik Erikson walked from his hometown, Karlsrühe, Germany, to Florence, Italy. He later said that he didn't trust any creative idea that hadn't occurred to its owner through walking. Other eminent Germans who did this were writer Johann Wolfgang von Goethe, philosophers Freidrich Nietzsche and Arthur Schopenhauer, and novelist Hermann Hesse.[201] Poet Ezra Pound wandered the south of France in the early 1900s, following the path of the French troubadours.

Exercise seems to be important among creators. Los Alamos was chosen as the site of the Manhattan Project because J. Robert Oppenheimer had a ranch nearby, where he would spend days in the wilderness with only a bottle of whiskey and his horse, exercising and thinking of physics. He loved the New Mexico desert as a place for contemplation and solitude.

It seems that many writers like to walk: Lexicographer Samuel Johnson liked to "compose, walking in the park."[202] Coleridge said he liked to think about writing while walking on uneven ground, climbing over rocks or breaking through the woods. Wordsworth liked to walk back and forth on a straight gravel sidewalk, and he and his sister Dorothy also tramped the hills, Dorothy taking notes while Wordsworth spun out images and words. Tennyson walked with his son, saying his latest poem out loud in rhythm, adding new lines as they seemed necessary. Novelist Charles Dickens walked around and around his house during the day, "smiting my forehead dejectedly." He also took long walks at night. A.E Housman, C.K. Chesterton and the Brontë sisters also paced and walked around and around a table as they planned their novels. Upton Sinclair said he wore a path six inches deep in the woods near where he composed one of his novels one summer. Jack Hodges, who collected these anecdotes, called it "ritualistic pacing."

Others run (poet Gary Gildner, novelist Haruki Murakama), wrestle (novelist John Irving), or engage in other physical activities that let them reach a state of creative fecundity.[203]

Exercise for a Group or for Staff Development

Take the Thoughtlogs, and set out on a walk. I've already told you about my little lunchtime poetry group of elementary kids meandering down Fifth Avenue to the

Metropolitan Art Museum, skipping on the octagonal sidewalk bricks, pointing out sights. These walks remain in my memory as a delight.

Exercise for an Individual

Take a walk. If you can't get yourself to do it, get yourself a personal trainer—a dog. Dogs need to go out. The saying goes among politicians in Washington, if you want a friend, get a dog. The same goes for exercise. You'll have both a friend and a willing but unobtrusive companion for your meditative walks.

Or, do some other exercise regularly. The endorphins of the aerobic exercise combine for fine creative thought.

Ways Teachers can Embed the Creative Practice of Exercise

Of course, the benefits of exercise are well known, and each school has expert practitioners in its physical education teachers. Consult your physical education colleague for ideas. Make sure that the students have active recess where they can play. Piggyback on their exercise periods. When they come in with their rosy cheeks and their excited mannerisms, do something creative.

CHAPTER 5

MY THOUGHTS AND INSIGHTS ON EXERCISE AS PART
OF THE CREATIVE PROCESS

Possibilities:

– How does exercise affect your creative thoughts?
– Why would exercise be so important to creators?
– Make an image (drawing, creative writing, music, photography, dance, diagram, skit, etc.) of some idea in this section.

THE QUEST FOR SILENCE

Some creators are extremely susceptible to noise and distraction, and seek to isolate themselves in a quiet place.[204] Silence is almost impossible to find or enforce. We live with background music, blasted and broadcast wherever we are. Many people cannot sleep without the television as white noise. The term *white noise* implies that the person is not concentrating on the sound, but that the sound is a comforting blanket that envelopes and pervades. In nature, of course, sounds also infuse the milieu and encompass throughout. Perhaps the quest for silence is not really a quest for silence, but a quest for the removal of certain kinds of noise—music, traffic, steps of others, and the like. Residents of Hawaii have complained that their silent nights had been invaded by tree frogs, which, in their mating, were so loud that the people were forced to retreat inside, put on television and music, and soundproofed their homes. However, the same species of frog is native to Puerto Rico, where their calls are welcomed.

Examples from Creators of the Quest for Silence

Writers especially seem to crave silence. To insulate himself from the noise outside and to work, Carlyle built a soundproof room, as did T.E. Lawrence. Somerset Maugham had the view to the Cote d'Azur in Paris bricked up so that he could concentrate; J.B. Priestley wrote with his back to a splendid view of the countryside; the children's author Roald Dahl closed the drapes and wrote in a small, dark room, which he called "a kind of womb."[205]

Family members had to pass by on tiptoe if their fathers were Dickens or Evelyn Waugh. Carl Sandberg's poet daughter, Helga Sandberg, said, in a television interview, that his children greeted him joyously when he would return from his frequent trips, and they would also be joyful when he left again because he demanded such silence that they could not be children.[206] In order to concentrate, in order to hear the inner voice, many creators must retire from sound. A friend lived next to a novelist in an old duplex in Ithaca, New York, a few years ago. Sound carried. The only sounds she could hear from next door, where there were two girls under six, was "Keep quiet!" from their yelling father, struggling to maintain his concentration. Absolute order was so necessary for Arnold Bennett that he inspected his study before settling down to write, to see whether the housekeeper had moved any of his objects even a fraction of an inch while dusting, and if his wife couldn't keep the dogs quiet, she would hear about it.

Of course, there is no such thing as silence, as demonstrated by avant-garde composer John Cage's widely-performed piece, *4'33"*, where the artist comes up to the piano and sits there silently for four minutes and thirty-three seconds, while the audience listens to the ambient sounds. Each performance, needless to say, sounds different, and the almost impossibility of finding silence is reinforced.

The appeal of retreats and colonies is that of peace and quiet away from the melee, so that the creative spirit can descend. At the famous Yaddo retreat center in Saratoga Springs, New York, lunch is delivered in a basket to the writers, musicians, and other artists hard at work in their cottages. Advertisements for such retreats promise remoteness, stillness, and solitude. The writer Annie Dillard wrote in *Holy the Firm* of going to a cabin in the woods and of isolating herself on an island in the Puget Sound.[207] The formation of retreats by enterprising or sympathetic entrepreneurs is a promise of quiet and freedom from distraction for writers tipping their heads sideways in order to hear the hushed footsteps of the muse.

Exercise for a Group or for Staff Development

Do the activities in silence. Discuss whether it is really silence you want, or certain kinds of noise. Quiet music? Sometimes I play new age or quiet classical music for activities in classes, and while most people are fine with it, one or two find the music distracting. This is especially true for music teachers, whose consciousness of music is acute.

Exercise for an Individual

Try to find silence. This is more difficult than it looks. A friend and I were driving in rural New Mexico, on our way to Georgia O'Keeffe's ranch, Abique, in the middle of the morning on a weekday. We gave ourselves a challenge. Try to find silence. We stopped our rental car frequently, pulling over on deserted highways, trying to listen for silence. We were unable. Those darned airplanes! Earplugs, anyone?

Ways Teachers can Encourage Silence

One of the best ways to encourage silence is to have students close their eyes and listen. This is how I used to encourage large groups of high school students to begin to write when I was Poet in the Schools for the National Endowment for the Arts. It most often worked. After the first giggles, that is.

MY THOUGHTS AND INSIGHTS ON THE QUEST FOR SILENCE
IN THE CREATIVE PROCESS

Possibilities:

- Do you need silence, white noise, or noise when you create? Explain.
- Describe a time you sought silence.
- Make an image ((drawing, creative writing, music, photography, dance, diagram, skit, etc.) of the quest for silence.

DIVERGENT PRODUCTION PRACTICE

Creativity is "in," and every creator is an expert. Unfortunately, much that is written about creativity focuses on the aspects of divergent production listed by Guilford in 1950 (see Chapter 1). Thousands of books and handbooks discuss divergent production. Researchers still give tests of divergent production to an experimental group and a control group, do some kind of teaching exercises, and then call the experimental group more *creative*. (I have asked editors of creativity journals who ask me to review articles not to send me any more articles to review that feature giving divergent production tests.) Why has the focus on divergent production been so prevalent over the past 60 years, why has it overtaken the field? The answer is simple. Divergent production is, indeed, a safe, reproducible, fun, and measurable way to focus on creativity. Researchers can have a working definition that can be worked with.

Those who would like to work creatively on environmental pollution could, ask group members list things that are green. This is called *brainstorming*. It is an open-ended activity that encourages *fluency* in creativity parlance. *Flexibility* training is also part of creativity enrichment. Teaching people to be flexible is asking them to come up with alternative ways of thinking. It's noncontroversial, and fun. An environmental group could classify the brainstormed ideas into categories.

Because this book focuses on alternative ways to enhance creativity, I only barely focus on divergent production here. Here's an exercise I use to teach people about the aspects of divergent production— fluency, flexibility, originality, elaboration, and transformation is to have the students brainstorm —say, the topic of Birds.

Fluency

Fluency means "how many," and the more the better. The group should divide into groups of four or five. "Brainstorm Birds," the leader says. The word *brainstorm* has made its way into the popular lexicon, and few people know its Guilfordian origins. The rules of brainstorming are that the participants must go as fast as they can listing ideas as they come to the mind — with a group member functioning as a recorder writing them down — participants should not judge of answers as in, "That's a really stupid idea." Or "No, that doesn't fit." or even "Will you explain that please?" The students make a long list of whatever people have come up with. The rules also include nodding and smiling, and not judging the quality of the responses. A long list ensues.

Flexibility

Flexibility is the ability to classify and categorize. Mary Meeker called it "set change," in her divergent production test, derived from Guilford's. To illustrate *flexibility,* ask them to look at the list and see how many different categories of answers with which they have answered. There may be *athletic teams* with the nicknames of birds, for example the St. Louis Cardinals, or the Baltimore Orioles. There may be *musical groups* named after birds, such as The Birds. There may be *species* of birds—robin, bluebird, owl, nightingale. There may be *food made from the flesh* of birds, turkey for Thanksgiving, turkey stuffing, chicken cacciatore, pheasant under glass. There may be *idiomatic sayings* using birds, such as "Don't put all your eggs in one basket," or "A bird in the hand equals two in the bush." Etcetera.

Originality

Originality means that no more than two people in thirty have thought of it. To illustrate *originality,* or *rarity,* ask them to look at their lists again and see which items they think are most original, most rare. They may have the name of a famous professional basketball player, "Larry Bird," or the name of a flower, "Bird of Paradise." If the unusual item does not appear in the lists of the other members in class, we call it original.

Elaboration

Elaboration is to focus on details, and to amplify, expand, and embellish. To illustrate *elaboration,* ask the students to take drawing paper and draw one of the most interesting items on their list. Each student individually draws something interesting. I ask them to draw it in some detail, and to invest it with individuality.

Transformation

Transformation is to alter, change, make over, or renovate. To illustrate *transformation,* as a collaborative assignment in divergent production, I ask them to exchange drawings, and to work on each other's drawings, changing them into a different drawing.

This simple exercise teaches the divergent production terminology, has group members experience what divergent production actually is and quickly illustrates the terms and their application to divergent production.

Another process that uses aspects of divergent production is the universally popular Creative Problem Solving Process (CPS). This originated at the State University of Buffalo, and is still taught nationally and internationally by their trainers and researchers. Businesses are fond of CPS, and many books have been written.[208] The Creative Problem Solving process alternates divergent production and convergent production. It has five steps, and each first uses brainstorming (divergent production) and then criteria finding (convergent production). Again, the point of this present book is not to elaborate on this, but just to present it as an alternate and popular general practice for creativity enhancement.

MY THOUGHTS AND INSIGHTS ABOUT DIVERGENT
PRODUCTION AS CREATIVITY

Possibilities:

- Why is divergent production so much fun?
- What experiences have you had with divergent production in the past?
- Make an image (image (drawing, creative writing, music, photography, dance, diagram, skit, etc.) of some idea in this section.

CREATIVITY AS THE PROCESS OF A LIFE

The creative process, ultimately, should be viewed as the province of every human being, and not just of the Einsteins, O'Keeffes, or Darwins of the world, or of those who make creative products such as music, or poems, or mathematical formulas. People's lives are their creative products. In the past few years, the creative process has gained cachet. Best-selling books have detailed how creativity is The Way.[209] Urban planning theorist Richard Florida described a "creative class," which is predicted to provide the most growth in jobs and salaries for the future. By mid-2010, Amazon.com listed 211,904 books that have to do with creativity. Google had 59,800,000 sources. The PyschInfo database had 18,468. Many of these tell people how to be more creative, or how to live creative lives.

Practices for enhancing creativity range from the strange (sitting beneath a pyramid) to the provocative (vision quest). Practices include visualization, imagery, metaphorization, chanting, and forming affirmations for personal empowerment. People caress sacred objects such as Zuni fetishes and they sit in a circle banging on drums. They croon in tones and dance like dervishes, seeking inner peace and the guidance for living a creative life. I have done many of these and enjoyed the workshops. Some of these practices have even made their way into my regular life. Creativity is intertwined with Creation, the spiritual, with a feeling of awe, of closeness to the essential. You may have tried some of these types of exercises, suggested throughout this book.

An outgrowth of the humanistic psychology movement and of the work of such humanistic psychologists as Carl Rogers, Abraham Maslow, and Fritz Perls, this quest for inner meaning has even made it to public television stations, where fundraising is led by former Detroit parochial high school guidance counselor, Wayne Dyer, who recently talked about inspiration.[210] Public television has also hosted the Bill Moyers *Creativity* series and the series written by Daniel Goleman called *The Creative Spirit*, both of which spoke to creativity as the process of a life.[211]

As mentioned above, Conference centers like The Open Center and the Omega Institute in New York, exist in most larger cities, and they offer creativity-focused sessions such as intensive journal workshops, dream, singing, improvisational theater, and dance workshops. Almost all the teachers of these workshops have written books that tell us how to enhance our creativity. Other, less exotic methods such as writing a spiritual autobiography (Dan Wakefield), upside down drawing (Betty Edwards), painting for healing (Rudolph Steiner followers and his Waldorf Schools), chanting (Robert Gass), engaging with the Mozart effect (Don Campbell), or dancing (Gabrielle Roth) are also employed in teaching people to be more creative, and thus to enhance the process of their lives.[212]

All have in common the probing of the inner psyche, making one's life a work of art, and the attainment of inner peace through self-therapy done by making creative products. All advertise "healing." Many have written books as experts on creativity.

Certain psychotherapists specialize in therapeutic interventions for those who are blocked in their creative pursuits. There are poetry therapists, art therapists, music therapists, dance therapists, drama therapists and the like, who have college degrees and who have taken tests for state-required licenses. They use the art to help their clients create metaphors for their troubles.

A metaphor stands for something else. It is symbolic. An image is a visual or aural representation that is metaphoric. Often these are coded. A code is a language that transmits a message. Creating metaphors and images that may be coded in ways the makers don't even realize, permits the emotion to be changed, to be released through a safe and therapeutic means.[213] The "talking therapy" is often not as effective as arts therapy, for the arts permit people to abstractly express themselves in the coded way that the arts allow. Doing the work of writing, making music, painting, drawing, dancing, acting—making an image from what is within—is itself therapeutic. Healing is present in creating a symbol or an image. Another whole industry has arisen in helping people overcome creative blocks.

A common intervention is the making of a mandala. Carl Jung, the original depth psychologist, began this practice with his neurasthenic, mostly female, analysands in Zurich. His books contain many such illustrations.[214] Other therapists have continued the practice, and so have teachers of creativity. The mandala is based on eastern thought, the idea that containing imagery within a circle can expose the inner universe of the mandala maker. Once I watched Buddhist monks work for a whole day on a sand mandala at the Cleveland Museum of Art. At an appointed time, they destroyed it, smearing the colorful sandy shapes into an amalgamation of grains. The destruction symbolized the transformation implicit in the image, and the transitoriness of human creativity.

Students can make personal mandalas, again, not for therapy, but for insight into the self. Educational psychologist Diane Montgomery has had high school students in our summer honors institutes make their own personal mandalas as a way to begin to go inward in her class, The Art and Science of Psychology. Jennifer Allen had her students in a graduate education educational psychology class make mandalas.

Mandala Exercise for a Group or an Individual.

The process is simple. Group members are led to deep breathing and to imagery by a relaxation exercise similar to the ones described in the inspiration section here. Simulated solitude is enforced; that is, no talking, silence, and, perhaps, soft music. As they enter the relaxed state, the leader asks them to let a word arise, and then to let an image that is a metaphor or symbol for the word come to the front. They should just let it arise and should not judge or censor the image. They focus on the image and let it take shape. What is its size, color, texture, smell, taste, shape? What is the background? The foreground? The context? What feelings and emotions arise from this image? This mental imaging should last a few minutes.

Then the group member draws a circle on a large piece of drawing paper. The circle is the boundary, but it is not rigid. Then the image should be drawn on the paper, and then colored in with patterns, images, and shapes. I have a large box of crayons, markers, and pens, which I pass out by the handfuls to each group member. If they need another color, they can get it from someone. Group members can go outside the line of the circle. The circle is the guideline.

The point is not to make a perfect image, nor to say, "I can't draw," but to create a symbol that is meaningful. The group members then display their mandalas on the room wall, without comment, and they may explain them if they wish, using the feeding back process described in Chapter 3. Mandala-making is an ongoing process in the creativity group, and mandalas may be edited, changed, re-drawn, re-cast, and quietly absorbed into consciousness. The mandala work connects you to a rich symbolic tradition practiced by native tribes, eastern societies, and indigenous designers.

Examples from Creators of Creativity as the Process of a Life

If the person is talented and trained in any domains the work produced as self-therapy, may become more. The work of the talented person transfigures and transforms other people's lives in its splendor, representation, and majesty, in its depiction of the human condition reaching toward the sublime. The history of talent domains abounds with examples: In visual arts, the story of Michelangelo painting the ceiling of the Sistine chapel in great emotional pain for the situations in his life is the example always cited. How the finger of God barely reaches the finger of man spoke to Michelangelo's own despair at the time, and to his desperate leap of faith, but anyone seeing this image can respond to its metaphors, symbols, and codes.

Ancient myths speak of the inspiration of the Muse, and of the power of Eros explain the impulse to make art in order to assuage feeling. Accounts of spiritual connections between the self, the work, and the emotion abound in the anecdotal literature. Plato wrote: "For the poet is a light and winged and holy thing, and there is no invention in him until he has been inspired and is out of his senses, and the mind is no longer in him; when he has not attained this state, he is powerless and is unable to utter his Oracles."[215] (By "poet," the Greeks meant all creators.)

Award-winning novelist Russell Banks said, "Storytelling has made it possible for me to make my life coherent to myself."[216] He believes he would have killed himself or have been killed if he hadn't written. "What would have happened to me is that I would have been stabbed to death in the parking lot outside a bar in Florida at 24, or something like that. I really believe that, actually. I think writing saved my life. I was so self-destructive, so angry and turbulent, that I don't think I could have become a useful citizen in any other way. So I don't think it worked as exorcism, or therapy, but I think it saved my life."

Doing the work itself is therapeutic. Van Gogh wrote to his brother Theo, "Either shut me up right away in a madhouse or else let me work with all my strength."[217] The dancer Isadora Duncan said, "My art is just an effort to express the truth of my Being in gesture and movement .... As an adolescent, I danced with joy turning to apprehension ... of the pitiless banality and crushing progress of life."[218] Singer-songwriter Rosanne Cash said about her music: "It's almost like a survival instinct, it's that primitive." She said that she has anxiety attacks, insomnia, develops eating problems and becomes irritable "if I ignore my work... it starts taking its toll in a very physical and mental way."[219] These three examples illustrate the importance to these talented people of using the symbol system of the domain to express complex internal feelings.

Creative expression is everywhere, and is, for most of us, lifelong. I hailed my 80 year old neighbor down in our shared driveway the other day to congratulate her, after I read in the paper that she had won best in show at the county fair for her quilts, as well as 5 other quilt prizes. "Do you sell them?" I said. "Oh no," she said. All my children, my grandchildren, my great grandchildren have them."

Personal transformation comes from work and intention, from the five core attitudes of openness to experience, risk-taking, tolerance for ambiguity, group trust, and self-discipline. It comes from working with Inspiration, Intuition, Insight, Imagination, Imagery, Improvisation, and Incubation. It comes from using solitude, ritual, meditation, silence, ritual, exercise, divergent production, and intention to make one's life one's creative product.

**MY THOUGHTS AND INSIGHTS ON CREATIVITY
AS THE PROCESS OF A LIFE**

Possibilities:

–   How is creativity part of the essence of your life?
–   How do you want to make creativity more a part of your life process?
–   Make an image (drawing, creative writing, music, photography, dance, diagram, skit, etc.)
    of an idea in this section.

CHAPTER 5

SUMMARY OF KEY POINTS

1. Creators often seek solitude in order to do their work.
2. Creators often use ritual before, after, or while doing their work.
3. Creators often use a form of meditation in doing their work.
4. Creators often precede or follow their work with exercise, especially walking.
5. Creators often seek silence in order to work.
6. Divergent production is a cognitive operation which may be helpful in generating ideas for creativity.
7. Creativity is the process of a lifetime.

CHAPTER 6

WORKING CREATIVELY WITHIN AN INSTITUTION

Often, teachers will feel that their personal attitude toward creativity enhancement in students is opposite to what the school itself projects. On the one hand, administrators and supervisors are touting "21st Century Skills," and on the other hand, they are demanding that teachers "teach to the test," raise test scores, focus on one-shot answers and not on deep understanding nor especially on self-expression. Even President Obama called for a focus on testing and measurement of achievement through testing. How can the teacher be creative when she/he is being inspected and expected to both focus on critical and creative thinking and make sure that students get good scores on standardized tests. The two are not mutually exclusive, and one could cite the research that says that a focus on understanding necessarily means that the test scores will rise.

The teacher's role is complex, and the profession of teacher demands extreme organization and a focus on outcomes as well as input. Teachers who have been able to focus on creativity have a belief that all students can be creative. They want their students to understand and not just parrot back "right" answers. They are able to differentiate the lessons and have a belief that students have a right to be taught at the readiness levels they possess. They like the students and take joy and delight in student expressiveness. They are not threatened by intuitive expressions, and are not threatened by open-ended assignments. Their students are permitted and encouraged to express their feelings, and to partner in the nature of assignments and products. The students feel valued and as if their opinions matter.

Administrators in the school that enhances creativity manage with understanding and value feedback. They view their jobs as facilitators for the main purpose of the school; to focus on creating a place where teachers and students can work on meaningful content through relationship. Administrators don't demean, dominate, or reject inspiration and feedback. They facilitate learning in its various forms. The school is a community where the administrator is privileged to work and to help the relationships fostered there—with students, teachers, parents, support staff. Respect is key. People love to come to school in this atmosphere, which is created by the administrator, who allays the suspicions of the central office, the teachers, the parents, the staff, and the students. Within the school setting, creativity can be squashed easily, and unheedingly. Here are some situational factors that can block or enhance creativity in the workplace.

SITUATIONAL FACTORS THAT BLOCK CREATIVITY

1. Overemphasis on verbally oriented, logical-analytical, cognitive ways of educating.
2. Tendency of teachers and parents to punish students who show evidence of emotional sensitivity, intellectual skepticism, playfulness, guessing, idealism.

143

3. Undue emphasis on practicality and usefulness.
4. Socio-economic blockages to produce conforming behaviors
5. Pressure tactics by parents and teachers.
6. Time limits.
7. Performance pressures.
8. Doing work one hates.
9. Organizational rules and regulations.
10. Overemphasis on neatness, cleanliness, order, discipline.
11. Lack of appreciation of the importance of creativity in everyday activities.

SITUATIONAL FACTORS THAT ENHANCE CREATIVITY

1. Group atmosphere that is playful, game like, non-competitive.
2. Group atmosphere that is not overly evaluative.
3. Conditions and materials that facilitate (make it easy).
4. Motivation that is related to the situation.
5. No time restraints, stopwatches, untimed condition.
6. Avoidance of interpretation.
7. Mutual trust.
8. Privacy.
9. Mild stress.
10. Process, rather than product orientation.
11. Solitude.
12. Meditation, thinking time.
13. Encouragement of intuitive perception.

Institutions often are viewed as preventing innovation and individual creativity, but there are ways to subvert this. One is to create your own classroom environment so that when students visit your "teacher cave," they know that creativity is encouraged here. The list below might help.[220]

– Keep in mind your philosophy of teaching. Maybe you need to revisit this philosophy, if you haven't worked on it since college or since you were interviewed for your job. How can your teaching space reflect your philosophy?
– Enter your space and try to see it with naiveté, as a newcomer coming in to the space would see it. What does the furniture, the walls, the decorations, the light, the floor say to the newcomer?
– Mentally go over and physically review the routines you have set up for teaching the various topics and subjects you teach. Are you organized for smoothness in transitions? What changes can you make in the tools you use, the materials you use, the furniture arrangements you use to make the routines more smooth? How can you organize the space so that the concepts in this book can be facilitated?
– Does everything in your environment support your creativity philosophy? Does it help you reach your goal for enhancing the students' creativity?
– Clear the clutter. Recycle what you haven't used in your teaching for awhile. Ask a colleague if he or she wants it. If not, donate it or discard it. Yes, that means those old overheads!

– Rearrange your wall displays for aesthetic appeal. Treat your room as an environment where pleasant experiences of learning can take place. Think of how your creativity can show in doing so. Try for balance, variety, harmony, and unity. Emphasize your love for your subject matter. Remember that student eyes wander and give their eyes something meaningful to land on.
– As the term goes on, add or remove things with forethought. Where do you place the announcements, schedules, logs, student work? How do you display it creatively. Consider your space an artistic composition and make it show who you are as a teacher.

How can these be Applied?

Yes, indeed, the students can begin to see the creative process as something that is, at base, part of their regular school experiences. My own teacher students have tried out the activities we have done in class, modifying them for their own use, for these suggestions are meant to be conceptual. I am not giving my students exercises to try on Monday morning, but a conceptual framework from which they can devise their own exercises, suitable for the age of the groups they are teaching. The *concept* of "risk-taking" is what is important; the *concept* of "inspiration" is important—to devise an activity at the application level that is suitable for the children one teaches is where the true creativity of the teacher comes in.

HOW TEACHERS CAN ENHANCE CREATIVITY IN CHILDREN

My book *Understanding Creativity*, contains a chapter on how teachers and parents can nurture creativity in children. I list 13 ways. These are as follows.[221]

1. Provide a Private Place for Creative Work to be Done

In a classroom, there are seldom private places where children can have privacy for doing creative work—reading, writing, drawing, composing, thinking. With fire safety laws and inspections, you probably can't build a loft in the early childhood/elementary room. Can you block off a private corner or section where children can feel a little apart? Beneath desks is good. Perhaps you can pitch a tent. Soft couches with frequently washed pillow covers might be tucked in somewhere. Leather for chairs or couches is good. As you picture the room in your mind (imagery, visualization), what can you do with it? Now all those hours of watching that design show on TV will pay off. Group the desks together to make tables. Push them together to make a circle so that all the children can see each other at all times. Use your own creativity to imagine a place where good schoolwork can get done and yet there is a place to read, to think, to draw. Use this place as a reward.

2. Provide Materials: Musical Instruments, Sketchbooks, Fabric, Paper, Clay

If the child has talent in a certain area, and if the parents do not have the means to develop that talent, the school has a responsibility to try to do so.

145

School materials should be made available to students when they are not being used for classes. Does your classroom have supplies, and are the children encouraged to be creative and free with these supplies? Creative teachers are known for their propensity to gather odd pieces and bits of materials and to recycle them for use in the classroom—oatmeal cartons, scraps of cloth, milk bottles, discarded containers—all become part of the teacher's supply closet. Old clothes are put into costume boxes for dramatic play; I know one teacher who haunts auctions and stays until the end when the leftovers are sold for a dollar. She has gathered many treasures this way, and they find their way into her classroom in craft projects, fantasy play, and even science fairs and invention conventions.

3. Encourage and Display the Child's Creative Work, but Avoid Overly Evaluating it.

Do you as a teacher know what creative talents your students have, and do you praise them for themselves; or are you in the dark? Many a child has stopped singing or drawing because of a teacher's or other students' sarcastic comments. We all know people—and perhaps we are among them— who, in giving a speech or demonstration, say, when illustrating something on the blackboard, "I'm not an artist, but ..." They make the drawing anyway, and most often we can tell what it is. The self-deprecating statement reflects on some past perceived failure in drawing.

Look back at your own childhood in school for a moment. Did a teacher or a peer say something to you that made you stop singing, stop drawing, stop writing, stop playing a sports game? Are you that same teacher, making similar, negative remarks to children? Remember that your remarks will live forever in those children's minds. As a teacher, I have to constantly remind myself that any remark I make will be magnified by my students and they will take it into themselves. A colleague told me this story the other day. He wrote on a student's paper that she was very talented in mathematics, and then forgot about the comment. A few years later, this student sent him a card, telling him that she was finishing studies for her Ph.D., and that his comment had given her the inner permission she needed to go to graduate school.

My graduate and undergraduate students have to do an individual creativity project as a final assignment in each of the creativity classes I teach. "But, I'm not creative," my graduate students often say. "I was going to drop the course the first night." One student made a timeline of her project, and for the first step in the project she spent some time asking friends and acquaintances "How am I creative?" She had no view of herself as being a creative human being. Who had done that to her?

4. Do your Own Creative Work, and let the Child See You Doing it

So what if you're a math teacher? Do your students know you are also a cabinetmaker? A painter? A writer? That you sew, or knit, or design boats? The wee bit of humanizing that such personal information does for you with your students can make a huge difference in their feelings of freedom of expression with you. Try it. Many say they aren't creative, but as adults, usually our creativity comes out in our hobbies, what we do when we are not teaching school. We are involved in cooking, crafts, building, refinishing of furniture, designing of exercise routines, local theater, church musical groups, and gardens. I just read in the paper that one of my colleagues whose office is down the hall baked an award-winning two-crust blueberry pie, and his wife, who is an adjunct professor, baked drop cookies that won.

What activities do you do in which you lose track of time, in which the activity is so challenging that it entices you, so pleasurable you can keep doing it for a long time? Everything from computer games to running comes up, but what inevitably is said, by someone or other, is that teaching well also gives them the pleasure of flow. That they love it when this happens in their classrooms. This leads me to think that teaching as a creative activity is under-valued by the curriculum designers who tell teachers they should teach this for fifteen minutes and this for ten minutes. The postmodern idea that teaching is meandering pleasurably with students in a river of knowledge where the ideas to be pursued arise from the context of the discussion supports the idea of teaching as a creative activity, but the curriculum planners who make teachers hand in detailed behavioral lesson plans and check off detailed task boxes, have taken the creativity out of what is essentially an art form, a skilled craft which is raised to the sublime when the teacher is really in there with the kids. I'll say it again: Teaching is an art.

5. Set a Creative Tone

When I was a school principal, I tried administratively to set the tone of the school as one of valuing creativity. When the long-awaited-six-months-late first copy of my novel arrived from my publisher one afternoon just before an assembly, I was so thrilled to see it that I jumped up and down and shouted, "Yes! Yes!" As the assembly began, one of the teachers announced to the group why I was behaving so strangely. Everyone applauded and laughed. They recognized that I was a struggling fiction writer as well as a principal. That administrators have lives that are creative is true.

Encourage teachers to set examples of creativity. This shows in their rooms. The halls should be filled with artwork; the bulletin boards should be replete with children's efforts. The rooms should be filled with learning centers, and every week there should be a performance or a class project. When I went to my granddaughter's high school open house recently, I noticed the humanities room with its photographs of classical statues, maps, books, and bright sculptures. In contrast, the math room was filled with the instructor's golf trophies and souvenirs of golf tournaments. Hmm. She's the golf coach?

The point I am trying to make here is that the school's atmosphere should show that the teachers are creative. Talk in the teacher's lounge may focus on movies, plays, books, travel, and musical performances, rather than on gossip about students and colleagues and complaints about how the union contract is being violated by the administration.

Teachers are interesting people, interested in creative things, and this shows in their interactive teaching, as well as in their out of school activities. Teachers may not have much money, but they raise great kids, who have probably seen more museums, battlefields, and national parks than other kids whose parents aren't teachers. When you enter a school you can tell within sixty seconds what the atmosphere is. And what the administrators and teachers value? Are there stern signs ordering visitors to go immediately to the principal's office, but no directions as to how to get there? Are there institutional lockers and gray walls? Is the school more like an army barracks than a joyful place where children learn to value their own creativity and humanity? Just go into any school and see what feelings and messages are conveyed by the walls, including things posted on the walls and in corridors, the signs, the windows, and the mood of the children themselves.

When I was a central office consultant for regional education offices, I had to go into many schools each day. This is when I learned this lesson about tone. The schools I enjoyed coming back to were the ones that conveyed a warm welcome, especially to children and frightened parents, but also even to central office administrators who are used to schools. I remember one school well. There was an actual waiting room near the entrance, with couches, lamps, magazines, and bulletin boards full of children's work. When parents came, they could visit with one other, share the gossip of the day, and feel as if they, too, had a place in the school their children attended.

6. Value the Creative Work of Others

Yes, I know you live in some small rural town miles from any real cultural life. I know. I grew up there, too. So why, in my very rural hometown of Ishpeming, Michigan, in the deep, dark woods, swamps, and lakes of the Upper Peninsula of Michigan, is there a project that has preserved the local history, the accomplishments and experiences of an entire community? Furthermore, why has that research been done by seventh graders? Called The Red Dust Project, a small junior high school collected oral histories of the local residents, and published them in an illustrated book. This project was initiated by a teacher.

Teachers are usually the most stable part of a community. Administrators often leave, and parents are involved only while their children are in school; but the teachers often stay for twenty, twenty-five, thirty (and in our state, what with the financial losses of the 2007–2009 Great Recession) thirty-five years. What the Red Dust teacher and her supportive administrator did, was simply teach the children to interview relatives and neighbors and then to write up the interviews. The children have had their work presented at the Smithsonian Museum. They have been featured on national television. All because one teacher had an idea that the creative people, all the people, in this small iron mining community should have their words and thoughts preserved.

Teachers in small towns across the land could initiate similar creative projects, even in remote areas where museums and live professional theater are far away.

7. Avoid Reinforcing Sex-Role Stereotypes

If your students don't have a family mythology that encourages cultural activities such as museums, concerts, or books, then your role is crucial. Field trips are a bother, yes, and busy school administrators often discourage efforts to take students to cultural events; but this should be a priority and a necessity, not a burden. Almost all of my graduate education classes take field trips. Sometimes I'm shocked that some of the teacher/students are visiting the local museums we visit for the very first time! A rule of thumb is that doing is better than passive viewing.

At the very minimum, each student should have a public library card, and each classroom should have a set of encyclopedias and enough computers with access to the Internet that there is little wait time. As teachers, you can model for your students that research and learning are part of your everyday life, as well. Here is what one writer I studied said about her favorite teachers:

> My "creative writing" teacher in high school was certifiably senile; I switched out of the class, an honors one, to a regular English class with a teacher who loved grammar. I hated grammar, but I learned there to love learning, and precision with words. Other memorable teachers were so only because they loved what they taught; thus I, who cannot draw a straight line with a ruler, recall the electricity and excitement of geometry class; I have a lot of buried knowledge and continuing fanaticism about Alexander the Great, because of an ex-jockey-turned-history-teacher whose love of that period of history sent me to the most obscure and advanced of resources, gave me a knowledge of library sources that has served me since, and gave me an absolute adoration of the whole process of knowledge: from the atmosphere in libraries to love of books for their new bindings and type as well as for their contents. It was not, I emphasize, WHAT these people taught, but HOW that worked the miracles–and I try to remember that every day I go into a classroom.

8. Avoid Reinforcing Sex-Role Stereotypes

> Many people who are homosexuals, regardless of gender, seem to have always known this about themselves, though some repress the knowledge. Whether homosexuals are more creative than other people is not known, but that stereo-type is reinforced by popular situation comedies, and reality shows. It would seem that creative fields are more open to sexual divergence.

But the point is not that there is a risk of homosexuality in being creative; the point is that following rigid sex role stereotyping limits creativity. In order to succeed in the world of visual arts, for example, a female artist needs to be willing to exhibit what are typically called masculine characteristics. The profession of artist demands an extraordinary commitment in terms of willingness to take rejection, to live in poverty, and to be independent. Those are typical traits of committed males, but not of committed females, who often choose careers as art educators and not as artists.

Female visual artists who reached eminence were often childless (e.g. Frida Kahlo, Georgia O'Keeffe, Lee Krasner), Judith Rothschild and Judy Chicago.[222] An eminent female visual artist who did have children, Alice Neel, was criticized by her sons for poverty and neglect, and by her granddaughter for the suicide of her abandoned daughter.[223] Girls' problems come when they try to reconcile the stereotypical paradox of the nurturing, recessive, motherly female with that of the unconventional artist. Boys' problems come when they try to reconcile the stereotypical paradox of the six shootin' muscle-flexing "real" man with that of a male who is sensitive, perceptive, and insightful. Teachers who reinforce such stereotypes may wound students forever.

9. Provide Private Lessons and Special Classes

The value of mentors is often spoken of. Researchers have gone so far as to say that a person will not reach eminence in science without apprenticing himself to a mentor scientist, without studying with the right teacher. Having the right teacher, who will have access to the right connections, is important.

The classroom teacher and the school counselor should seek to to provide the talented child and the parents with information about suitable mentors or other opportunities. While the relationship between mentor and mentee is deeply personal and cannot be legislated or mandated, efforts can be made. Schools must also play a part in the development of talent, helping to find private teachers and mentors for talented children from families without financial resources. Petitioning local clubs and organizations to pay for lessons for a struggling but talented child can best be done by the school (anonymously, of course). A teacher paid for the room and board of one of our students at a summer institute. She did it so quietly that I never learned her name, but the child's life was changed by the experience.

10. Use Hardship to Teach the Child Expression through Metaphor

Try to notice and be sensitive to the personal situations of the children you teach. Ban the term "broken home" from your vocabulary. Don't be under the impression that a child will not be creative because he is poor or disheveled. A former student of mine, a bilingual Spanish/English teacher, discovered the creativity of a boy living in extreme poverty because he was always reading. She took photographs of him reading in the bus line, in the lunchroom, in the hallways, in math class, on the playground. She then identified him as having potential writing talent by asking him to write stories, which were extraordinary blends of Mexican and Central American mythological characters. A recent class discussion featured a teacher's tale about a talented boy who loved to write. He had his classmates in sixth grade weeping with a story about his dead mother. He had lived in 11 foster homes that year, and before the end of the year was moved again--out of the district where my student teaches. She had, however, planted in him the idea that his work was able to move people, by just having him read his story out loud in an atmosphere of trust and acceptance.

11. Discipline and Practice are Important

Teachers of the talented especially must realize that such children are often overly praised and rewarded just for possessing the talent. Teachers of the artistic disciplines—the visual arts, writing, music, dance, theater—know what it takes to realize that talent, but often such talented students are not given special help by the school. They are instead thrown in with far less talented students in art, music, math, and science. This would never happen in athletics, where talented students are permitted to advance according to their abilities, and compete with people at their own levels of expertise. Accurate and qualified feedback is important in the development of talent, and the child should have access to people who have some expertise. Mentoring is important.

Another challenge is not to counter-identify. Often the teachers of talented students are almost as jealous and anxious as parents are. Case in point, the war between the cheerleading coach and the choir director on the television series, *Glee.* When teachers counter-identify, they feel horrible when the student doesn't perform or when the child makes a mistake. They are as narcissistic as the parents and coaches described by Tofler and deGeronimo in their book about Achievement-by-Proxy.

Not to overly identify with the talented student is particularly difficult when the teaching relationship becomes a coaching relationship. Teachers can be temperamental and cruel, pushing hard until the students hate the field. A former swimmer once told me that he would never swim again, never go near a pool, because his college coach demanded that he swim seven hours a day in order to improve his time a few seconds. He fears that swimming will never again be a pleasure for him. Judith Kogan also spoke to this difficulty while describing idiosyncratic, belittling, and demanding music teachers at Juilliard. One of my students just recently shared that his talented football player son was so burnt out by his Mid-American Conference football experience and his coach that he rejected overtures by the NFL.

Tofler and DiGeronimo warned parents against permitting their children to be with instructors who want to achieve by proxy. They said parents should avoid the "Win-at-any-cost Instructor"; "The Verbal Batterer"; and "The Parent Substitute." If their talented child is to spend any amount of time away from home, they also recommend that parents look into the coach's record with regard to harassment or sexual abuse of minors. They cited thirty cases of coaches who were arrested or convicted of sexually abusing children in sports.

12. Allow the Child to be "Odd"; Avoid Emphasizing Socialization at the Expense of Creative Expression

The schools often see their major roles as socializing children so they fit into a mold and become acceptable to the society that the schools serve. Many educators consider socialization to be as important as teaching the children to read, write and figure, for this is what the "real world" demands. But creative people are often at odds with the world and are prickly, rebellious, and nonconforming. (Note: Often their nonconforming is actually conforming, but conforming to a stereotype similar to how they perceive creative people to behave.) Often creative students act out in class, are argumentative, and consciously underachieve; that is, they do well in classes they like, but don't care about classes they don't like, or see as irrelevant to their futures. Often creative students stereotype their teachers by age and by looks.

One summer I was teaching a fiction writer's workshop to a group of specially selected teenagers from throughout the state of Ohio. One of the young women was quite surly as she looked at me in my middle age, with my conservative haircut, my comfortable, but rather rumpled summer clothes. When I mentioned that one of the guest readers I was going to bring in was poet Nick Muska, a good friend of mine, who had written a theater piece about Jack Kerouac, called *Back to Jack*, this young woman's attitude changed. She was from Toledo, Nick's town, and knew him from the poetry scene in that city. "*You* know Nick Muska?" she said incredulously. "Yes. We've been friends for many years," I said simply. "But I *love* Nick Muska!" she said. And she brought in her personal collection of Jack Kerouac's books to show me the very next session.

Some creative students may need therapy. They view themselves as too different, too creative, too cool for anything the schools might have to offer. Often their rebelliousness carries over to the therapist's office as well. One teenage creative writer I know said she sat in stubborn silence when she was sent to a therapist. Another creative child who was videotaped for a case study by one of my students said that even though her mother made her go to therapy because of her nonconforming behavior, she didn't benefit because she felt so much smarter than the therapist.

13. Use Humor and Get Creativity Training

Besides enjoying and being frustrated by that child's sense of humor, we as teachers should monitor our own ways of dealing with creative children. Do we enjoy children? Do we laugh with children (or at them, when appropriate)? Do we have fun with children? In other words, is being with creative children a pleasure? found that elementary school teachers use more humor than junior high teachers.[224] Junior high teachers most frequently use funny comments, funny stories, and jokes, though male junior high teachers told jokes more often. But the alarming thing is that junior high, high school, and college teachers used hostile and tendentious humor such as ridicule and sarcasm much more often than elementary teachers. In fact, nearly half the humor used by these teachers of older students was sarcastic. Humor used in a hostile manner can be hurtful to children. Sarcasm is not what is wanted here, but rather humor used in gentler ways to create a happier, more relaxed classroom, and thus help students have positive attitudes towards learning. Humor contributes to the development of creative thinking, and one can see why, for non-hostile humor creates the feeling of freedom and play that is necessary for creative thinking.

Get creativity training. If school districts are serious about effectively teaching creative thinking, they must provide the necessary backup training. There are many commercial programs available and many trained people who can provide creativity training to school districts. School districts also should provide the rigorous instruction in the fields in which the creativity training can be applied. Many opportunities for teaching students to be more creative exist. Every school has experts who can help the student who is creative in some domain to be nurtured in that domain.

Many people do not believe that the school is the place to work to enhance student creativity, but the recommendations of the 21st Century Skills movement say they are wrong.

The practice of all of these, in raising and teaching the young, can aid in personal transformation, and in creativity as the process of a life. For example, take number 9: "If hardship comes into your life, use it positively to teach the child self-expression through metaphor." If trouble comes into life try to make (as in create) something of it through the arts. Release of emotion through the arts is often indirect, perhaps more therapeutic than therapy itself. The depth psychologists speak of the fire within that is turned into an image, a thing out there. Teachers should provide sketchbooks. Provide journals. Provide music lessons. Provide privacy. They should resist interpretation.

Whether or not the requisite talent is present, at the very minimum, adults could try to notice and be sensitive to the emotional situations of the children with whom they come into contact The group of young writing prodigies with whom I worked back in New York City indicated that writing was, for them, a way of finding out what they think, and a way of expressing emotions. One of them said, "I write to find out what I think." They were 8 years old. One of them, Bobby Lopez, went on to win a Tony for writing the lyrics of *Avenue Q*, an award-winning Broadway show.

What I call predictive behaviors are shown early and often. Young artists draw. Young singers sing. Young actors have backyard or attic theaters. Teachers notice. Teachers are the "Sun of School" in my Pyramid of Talent Development (Chapter 1), and they are a very hot and powerful sun indeed.

How Administrators can Enhance Creativity in their Workplaces

But the teacher is not alone. An institution is formed by savvy and supportive administrators. Here is an essay by one of my students, a school administrator in the Big Walnut Local School District in Ohio, a district that ranks statewide as Excellent With Distinction.

School districts should try to provide professional development in creative thinking and in the creative process. The call for more creativity in the schools often goes unanswered, as fear of the implications for test scores and fear of being evaluated take precedence. The core belief that all students are creative and the core belief that students can grow through the emphasis of the five core attitudes is primary. Valuing creativity in problem finding and problem solving will spread throughout the institution. The embedding of the seven I's, and the general practices will help to foster innovation in thinking and being and will encourage independent thinking through a process that values independent thought.

Table 6.1. How administrators can enhance creativity in their workplace

---

How Administrators can Enhance Creativity in their Workplace

Steve Butler
(used with permission)

In day-to-day practice, the process of group creativity by teachers, administration, and other staff can serve directly to provide the best possible learning opportunities for our students. As Big Walnut Schools encourage collaboration among school buildings, grade levels, and/or subject teams, we can teach staff to practice the core attitudes of creativity.

Demonstration and participation are, by my way of thinking, the best way to teach. I believe that practicing the five core attitudes is the most beneficial method of learning a collaborative, creative process. Such a process can be very useful in school administration, teacher lesson planning, business planning, comedy writing, song writing, and other areas of group interaction and creativity. Through the core attitudes of *naiveté* (openness), *self-discipline*, *risk-taking* (courage to stumble and try, try again), and *group trust*, a cohort of people can create and grow, sharing the ideas, skills, and abilities of all. Adding *tolerance for ambiguity*, the fifth core attitude, changes things a bit for me. While it creates a chance for a variety of thoughts, options, and opinions, it also lengthens the process and makes group decisions harder. Is that good or bad? Depending on time constraints and flexibility of the decision, it could be either!

Perhaps group trust may need to be developed first. To do this, a session in which the future participants meet to set group expectations, standards, or attitudes is vital. For example, in our administrative team at Big Walnut, the "norms" (ground rules or habits which govern the group) include the following:[225]

- We will presume positive intentions.
- We will give and receive confidentiality.
- We will be supportive of team decisions.
- We will be prepared for proactive, inquiry-based problem solving.
- We will celebrate our successes.
- We will stay focused on our goals.
- We will have fun and laughter.

Such norms should be developed by each team to meet its needs and purpose. Once norms are in place, openness, risk-taking, and tolerance for ambiguity will find their place in a safe and secure environment, and self-discipline will take place as respect for others in the group requires each member to be involved in the team. I would get the group together to develop norms. Depending on the members there may already be a good bit of trust, or total trust, or no trust.

While I am generally not interested in "icebreakers" and "warm-up" activities, this may be a time when some are necessary. With administrative decisions and classroom lesson planning requiring final action, I think a group will be inspired to

---

work together, and in working together, trust will likely grow. If not, team membership may need to be adjusted over time. I would continue to stress, that the outcomes of the group activities must be timely, but that flexibility is also possible through time.

This week I received an e-mail from a colleague. The e-mail included information on a book entitled *How to Think Like Leonardo da Vinci*, by Michael J. Gelb, and a response-inspired by the book. The response, "How to Prevent Another Leonardo da Vinci," in a blog by Kris Bradburn, outlined points which teachers and others must do to "kill each trait that may yield another Da Vinci." Interesting to me was the fact that an insatiably curious approach to life (naiveté), testing of knowledge through experience (risk-taking), energy and desire to focus intensely (self-discipline), and acceptance of ambiguity each were mentioned in these writings.

Finally, I want to discuss the importance of solitude (mentioned in Chapter 5) as an aspect of the creative process, and tell how it fits very neatly into the group process. Prior to any group meeting, and with enough time for individuals to reflect on upcoming topics, an agenda for the meeting needs to be shared. This allows members of the team an opportunity to ruminate on the items to be discussed, not to formulate "etched in stone" answers, but to be prepared and able to participate in "brainstorming," discussion, and decision-making.

Thus, the nurturing of creativity can be a partnership. Along the way, the members of the group might also make the core attitudes, seven I's, and general practices part of their own personal lives. Individuals can also enhance their own creativity, by trying the exercises described here.

SUMMARY OF KEY POINTS

1. Educational institutions can be places where creativity can flourish.
2. Certain situational factors can enhance or stifle creativity.
3. Teachers can foster creativity in many ways.
4. Administrators can foster creativity in many ways.

CHAPTER 6

MY THOUGHTS AND INSIGHTS ON THE IDEAS IN THIS CHAPTER

Possibilities:

- What situational factors are operant in your own workplace to either enhance or discourage creativity?
- Which two of the 13 suggestions for teachers speaks to you?
- How do you as a teacher or administrator enhance creativity within your institution?
- Make an image (drawing, creative writing, music, photography, dance, diagram, skit, etc.) of some idea in this chapter.

APPENDIX A:
PIIRTO PYRAMID OF TALENT DEVELOPMENT

APPENDIX A

Here is the Piirto Pyramid, my theoretical framework for how creative talent develops.

The Piirto Pyramid of Talent Development

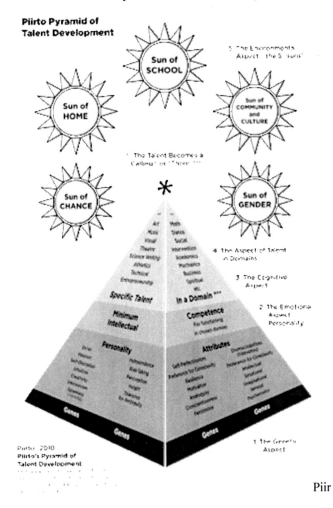

Figure 2. Piirto pyramid of talent development.

THE PIIRTO PYRAMID OF TALENT DEVELOPMENT:

A CONCEPTUAL FRAMEWORK

"The 'Pyramid' is excellent—a compact, eloquent, graphic synthesis. "
— Frank Barron (one of the original creativity researchers in the 1950s, personal communication to the author)

Note: I published my first version of the Piirto Pyramid in 1994. Over the years it has evolved thanks to talks and critiques from friends, students, and colleagues. My model of the human and the developmental influences on that person is sometimes humorously called the Piiramid of Talent Development. (With thanks to my friend Michael Piechowski for the wit.) This model has guided my work on talent in domains. It is a contextual framework that considers the 4 P's of creativity— person, process, and product, as well as press, or environmental factors. Article expositions were in Piirto (1994; 1995a, b; 1998; 1999a; 2001; 2004, 2007, 2008a, b, c, d; 2)

The following are the basic assumptions of the Piirto Pyramid

1. Creativity is domain-based.
2. Environmental factors are extremely important in the development of talent.
3. Talent is an inborn propensity to perform in a recognized domain.
4. Creativity and talent can be developed.
5. Creativity is not a general aptitude, but is dependent on the demands of the domain.
6. Each domain of talent has its own rules and ways in which talent is developed.
7. These rules are well-established and known to experts in the domain. Talent is recognized through certain predictive behaviors. Coaches of athletics know this (body type, dexterity, physicality, etc.). Musicians know this (matching pitch, dexterity, tonal quality of voice, etc.). Each domain has its predictive behaviors that are, for the most part, evident in childhood.

1. *The Genetic Aspect*

We begin with our genetic heritage. We have certain predispositions, and studies of twins reared apart have indicated that, as we become adults, our genetic heritage becomes more dominant. Our early childhood environment has more importance while we are children than when we are adults. As we age, we become more like our genetic relatives.

2. *The Emotional Aspect: Personality Attributes*

Many studies have emphasized that successful creators in all domains have certain personality attributes in common. These make up the base of the model.

These are the affective aspects of what a person needs to succeed and they rest on the foundation of genes. Among these are androgyny, creativity, introversion, intuition, naiveté or openness to experience; overexcitabilities, passion for work in a domain, perceptiveness, persistence, preference for complexity, resilience, self-discipline, self-efficacy, and volition, or will.

These attributes were originally from literature review of studies on the talented and creative. I have independently confirmed most of them with my own research on talented adolescents.

This list is by no means discrete or complete, but shows that creative adults achieve effectiveness partially by force of personality. Talented adults who achieve success possess many of these attributes. One could call these the foundation, and one could go further and say that these may be innate, although to a certain extent they can also be developed and directly taught.

What does it mean to have such personality attributes? What is personality and how does it contribute to effectiveness? Personality is, fortunately or unfortunately, an area in which there are many competing theories. Defined simply as "the set of behavioral or personal characteristics by which an individual is recognizable," with synonyms such as individuality, selfhood, and identity, personality theory can be psychoanalytic (Ego psychology, object relations, transpersonalism); behavioral or cognitive (quantitative studies using factor analysis or humanistic (using phenomenology, existentialism, gestalt, humanistic, and transpersonal theories). Personality is sometimes equated with character, directing how one lives one's life. The personality attributes mentioned here have been determined by empirical studies of creative producers—mostly adults, but in some cases, adolescents in special schools and programs. Many of the personality attributes from studies used have focused on the Myers-Briggs Type Indicator, based on the Jungian theory of personality.[226] The Cattell 16 Personality Factors Inventory, The Eysenck Personality Inventory, the Gough Creative Personality Inventory, the California Psychological Inventory, the Minnesota Multiphasic Psychological Inventory, and others have also been used in studies cited here.

3. The Cognitive Aspect

Although the cognitive dimension in the form of an IQ score has been over-emphasized, it is certainly essential. IQ is best seen as a minimum criterion, mortar and paste, with a certain level of intellectual ability necessary for functioning in the world. Having a really high IQ is not necessary for the realization of most talents. Rather, college graduation seems to be necessary (except for professional basketball players, actors, and entertainers), and most college graduates have above average IQs but not stratospheric IQs.

4. The Talent Aspect: Talent in Domains

The talent itself —inborn, innate, mysterious—should also be developed. It is the tip of the Piirto Pyramid. Each comprehensive high school has experts in most of the talent domains that students will enter. These include mathematics, visual arts, music, theater, sciences, writing and literature, business, entrepreneurship, economics, athletics, dance, the spiritual and theological, philosophy, psychology, the interpersonal, and education. These are all well-defined academically, and if a person has a talent in a domain, he or she can find people who can advise how to enter study in any of them.

When a child can draw so well she is designated the class artist, or when an adolescent can throw a ball 85 miles an hour, when a student is accused of cheating on her short story assignment because it sounds so adult, talent is present. Most talents are recognized through certain predictive behaviors, for example voracious reading for linguistically talented students, and preferring to be class treasurer for mathematically talented students. These talents are demonstrated within domains that are socially recognized and valued, and thus may differ from society to society.

(For example, hunting ability—acuity of eye combined with a honed instinct for shooting and a knowledge of animal habitat—is presently not as socially recognized and valued in western society as is verbal ability—a sensitivity to words and their nuances as expressed through grammatical and idiomatic constructions on paper. In the past, hunting ability was valued much more than verbal ability. Nevertheless, the genetic talent to hunt is still born in certain children, regardless of whether urbanites view such talent as anomalous.)

5. Environmental "suns"

These four levels on this imagistic pyramid could theoretically be called the individual person.

In addition, everyone is influenced by five "suns," which may be likened to certain factors in the environment. The three major suns refer to a child's being (1) in a positive and nurturing **home** environment, and (2) in a **community and culture** that conveys values compatible with the educational institution, and that provides support for the home and the school. The (3) **school** is also a key factor, especially for those children whose other "suns" may have clouds in front of them. Other, smaller suns are (4) the influence of **gender,** for there have been found few gender differences in personality attributes in adult creative producers; and (5) what **chance** can provide. The presence or absence of all or several of these make the difference between whether a talent is developed or whether it atrophies.

Unfortunately, it could be said that when a student emerges into adulthood with his or her talent nurtured and developed it is a miracle, because there are so many influences that encroach on talent development. We all know or remember people with outstanding talent who did not or were not able to use or develop that talent because of circumstances such as represented by these suns.

For example, a student whose home life contains trauma such as divorce or poverty may be so involved in that trauma that the talent cannot be emphasized. In the absence of the home's stability and talent development influence (e.g. lessons, atmosphere for encouragement), the school's, and the teacher's or coach's role becomes to recognize the talent and to encourage lessons, mentors, or special experiences that the parents would otherwise have provided had their situation been better. The "suns" that shine on the pyramid may be hidden by clouds, and in that case, the **school** plays a key role in the child's environment.

As another example, in a racist society, the genes that produce one's race are acted upon environmentally; a person of a certain race may be treated differently in different environments. The **school** and the **community and culture** are important in developing or enhancing this genetic inheritance. Retired U. S. general Colin Powell has said that he entered the army because he saw the military as the only **community and culture** in a racist society where he would be treated fairly, where his genetic inheritance of African American would not be discriminated against, where he could develop his talents fully.

Although many **gender** differences are genetic and innate, gender's influence on talent development is also environmental. Boys and girls may be born with equal talent, but something happens along the way. Few personality attributes show significant gender differences [except for Thinking and Feeling on the Myers-Briggs Type Indicator (MBTI) and "tender mindedness" on the 16 Personality Factors Inventory (16 PF)]. Similarly; few intelligence test scores show significant gender differences (though boys consistently score higher in spatial ability), and so we should look at how the environment influences the development of talent according to **gender**.

The importance of **chance**, or luck, cannot be overemphasized. As the principal of a school in New York City, I received many calls from casting agents and producers wanting to look at our bright children for possible roles in movies, television, and theater. These children had the luck of being born in and living in a center for theatrical activity. I'll warrant few school principals in, say, Kansas City or Seattle Washington, get the weekly and even daily calls I got from casting agents.

The influence of **chance** comes when a person happens to meet someone who can connect him or her to another person who can help or influence his or her opportunities to interact with the field or domain. The Sun of **Chance** has clouds over it when a talented adolescent in a rural high school does not get the counseling needed to make a college choice that will enhance a career. Chance can be improved by manipulating oneself so that one can indeed be in the right place at the right time.

6. The Thorn— Feeling the Call

However, although absolutely necessary, the presence of talent is not sufficient. Many people have talent, and are not interested in doing the work necessary to develop it. Emotional investment is the impetus for one acquiring the self-discipline and capturing the passion and commitment to develop the talent. It takes obsession and dedication and energy to chase an idea for years, working on it with a sense of purpose and sacrifice, even in the face of rejection from others. To continue the pursuit of one's creative obsession requires what is commonly called a vocation or a call. Thus I put an asterisk, or "thorn" on the pyramid to exemplify that talent is not enough for the realization of a life of commitment. Without going into the classical topics of desire, emotion, wisdom, or soul, suffice it to say that the entire picture of talent development ensues when a person is pierced or bothered by a thorn, the daimon, as Carl Jung called it, the acorn, as James Hillman called it, that leads to commitment.[227]

One of the definitions of *gift* comes from Old French for *poison* and this is what the talent that bothers may become to a person if the person doesn't pay attention to it. As well as a joy it is a burden. As well as a pleasure it is a pain. However, the person who possesses the talent also must possess the will and fortitude to pursue the talent down whatever labyrinth it may lead.

APPENDIX B:
FOCUS QUESTIONS FOR CLASSES USING
THIS BOOK

FOCUS QUESTIONS FOR CLASSES USING THIS BOOK

CHAPTER 1: CREATIVITY FOR 21ST CENTURY SKILLS:

1. Critique the chart comparing the 21st century skills with the skills of the Five Core Attitudes, Seven I's, and General Practices.
2. Fill out your own Pyramid of Talent Development, based on the figure in Appendix A.
3. Comment on the personality attributes on the bottom of the Pyramid.
4. Comment on the cognitive aspect on the Pyramid.
5. Comment on the talent in domains on the Pyramid.
6. Comment on the Environmental Suns on the Pyramid.
7. Discuss creativity training you have experienced.
8. What is your creative process when you are working on something?
9. What does your place of work do to help you be creative?
10. What is your "thorn"?
11. Discuss your motivation for creating.
12. Discuss your training, study, and development in a domain.
13. Make an image (drawing, creative writing, music, photography, dance, diagram, skit, etc.) of some aspect in this chapter.

CHAPTER 2: FIVE CORE ATTITUDES

1. Discuss how practice made for automaticity in the expertise you have acquired.
2. How does self-discipline figure into your own creative life?
3. Describe how travel has contributed to your sense of naivete or openness to experience.
4. Discuss how openness to experience has figured into your own creative life.
5. Discuss how you or someone you know has displayed "creative courage," or risk-taking.
6. What keeps you from taking risks?
7. How does your own tolerance for ambiguity affect your decisions?
8. What experience with ambiguity has stuck with you?
9. Describe a time when a lack of group trust stifled your creativity.
10. Describe a time when group trust enhanced your creativity.
11. Make an image (drawing, creative writing, music, photography, dance, diagram, skit, etc.) of some aspect in this chapter.

CHAPTER 3: THE SEVEN I'S: INSPIRATION

1. Describe a time when the muse visited you.
2. Describe how the Greek definitions of types of love resonate with you, with examples of each.
3. List memories of nature from your past and your feelings about them.
4. Describe a time when nature inspired you.

5. How did the inspiration of transcendent experience section resonate with you with regard to your own creativity?
6. Why are people afraid of transcendent experience as inspiration for creativity?
7. Describe a time when a substance affected your creativity.
8. Why are people afraid of mentioning the inspiration of substances as a source of creativity?
9. How have the works of the people in your creative field inspired you?
10. Describe a time someone else's creative work transported you.
11. What is your recurring dream and how does it affect your creativity?
12. How do you apply or use the insights from your dreams?
13. Be particular and describe (re-see) a travel experience.
14. How does armchair traveling (television, books) inspire you?
15. Be particular and describe (re-see) an experience that was traumatic for you.
16. How does your reading, game-playing, television-viewing affect your view of the tragedies in the world?
17. Why should being thwarted inspire creativity?
18. Tell a story about you or someone you know creating because of frustration.
19. How does injustice inspire you?
20. What does creativity have to do with social justice and injustice?
21. Make an image (drawing, creative writing, music, photography, dance, diagram, skit, etc.) of some aspect in this chapter.

CHAPTER 4: THE SIX OTHER I'S

1. What is the difference between imagery and imagination?
2. Make an image (drawing, creative writing, music, photography, dance, diagram, skit, etc.) about the "I" of Imagery.
3. What would the world be like without imagination?
4. When you are imagining things, how do you feel?
5. Describe a time when you had a hunch and it paid off.
6. What does Davis mean when he says "If it lasts through the night it will last forever"?
7. Describe a time when you incubated a creative solution.
8. How does incubation work in the mind and body?
9. Describe the physical and mental circumstances of your last insight. What was it about?
10. What does insight have to do with creativity?
11. List and reflect on some times when you improvised.
12. How difficult is improvisation?
13. Make an image (drawing, creative writing, music, photography, dance, diagram, skit, etc.) of some idea in this chapter.

CHAPTER 5: GENERAL PRACTICES IN THE CREATIVE PROCESS

1. Describe the last time you had solitude. How did you feel?
2. Why is solitude necessary for some creators?

3. What rituals do you practice before or during the times you are creating?
4. Describe the rituals you have observed others performing during ceremonial events.
5. What is your experience with meditation?
6. Why would meditation enhance the creative process?
7. How does exercise affect your creative thoughts?
8. Why would exercise be so important to creators?
9. Do you need silence, white noise, or noise when you create? Explain.
10. Describe a time you sought silence.
11. Why is divergent production so much fun?
12. What experiences have you had with divergent production in the past?
13. How is creativity part of your life process?
14. How do you want to make creativity more a part of your life process?
15. Make an image (drawing, creative writing, music, photography, dance, diagram, skit, etc.) of some idea in this chapter.

CHAPTER 6: WORKING CREATIVELY WITHIN AN INSTITUTION

1. What situational factors are operant in your own workplace to either enhance or discourage creativity?
2. Which two of the 13 suggestions for teachers speaks to you?
3. How do you as a teacher or administrator enhance creativity within your institution?
4. Make an image (drawing, creative writing, music, photography, dance, diagram, skit, etc.) of some idea in this chapter.

NOTES

1 This book is a longer exposition of the last chapter of my book, *Understanding Creativity* (Piirto 2004). The principles explicated here have appeared in various articles and chapters I have written, as well, and in various workshops I have given over the years (Piirto, 1999b, Piirto 2005a, b, 2007c, 2008c, 2008f, 2009d, 2010a).

2 Meeker, 1977.

3 Guilford, 1950; 1967.

4 These are common strategies used in classrooms and workshops to help people be more fluent, flexible, elaborative, and the like. SCAMPER stands for S-ubstitute, C-ombine, A-dapt, M-odify, P-ut to other purposes, E-liminate, R-earrange. It was developed by a former school superintendent and prolific writer of strategy books for elementary teachers, Bob Eberle.

5 The Creative Problem Solving Institute: http://www.creativeeducationfoundation.org

6 www.21stcenturyskills.org. See Trilling and Fadel, 2009.

7 Guilford, 1950, p. 454.

8 Palmer has written a very popular book, and created a program focusing on the inner life of teachers, called *The Courage to Teach.*

9 See Kaufman & Baer, 2004, for an edited book which considers several domains, with essays written by psychologists and educators. See the edited books on creative writing, (Kaufman & Kaufman, 2009).as well (Kaufman,

10 See Piirto, 1992, 1994, 1998, 1999, 2004, 2008, 2009, in press.

11 One of the most influential articles on that topic was poet Brewster Ghiselin's, written in 1952, as an introduction to his anthology, *The Creative Process,* where he collected thoughts by creative people describing what they do before, during, and after they create. Brewster Ghiselin was Calvin Taylor's colleague at the University of Utah. Taylor was a psychologist who was a pioneer in creativity studies, who held seminal conferences on creativity in the early 1950s. Ghiselin came to creativity studies through his friendship with Taylor.

12 Cf. Perkins, 1981; Sternberg & Lubart, 1999.

13 Freud (1908/1976), Jung (1923/1976), and Hillman (1975).

14 Plato, *Dialogues*; Calame, 1995.

15 "Right-brain" is shorthand for someone who is more creative. Cf. Pink, 2006.

16 In the course we use my books as primary texts. Piirto, 2004; 2007b.

17 Jung, 1933, p. 169.

18 Jung. Ibid.

19 Stambler, 2008, p. 52; http://www.achievement.org/autodoc/page/jon0int-3

20 Amabile, 1996. Theresa Amabile, a social psychologist, has done some of the major work on motivation for creativity. Her books assert that motivation is an important key to creativity. Amabile came up with a Venn diagram, and said that creativity takes place where these three intersect: domain skills, creative thinking and working skills, and intrinsic motivation.

21 Rothenberg, 1989.

22 Callahan, 1997, p. 220.

23 Clapton, 2007, p.

24 "Einstein, God, and the Universe" radio program. *The Best of Our Knowledge.* Public Radio International, January 12, 2009.

25 Here are examples of research support for the personality attributes: *androgyny* (Barron 1968b; Csikszentmihalyi, Rathunde, and Whalen 1993; Piirto & Fraas, 1995; Piirto & Johnson, 2004); *creativity* (Renzulli, 1978); *imagination* (Dewey, 1934; Langer, 1957; Plato; Santayana, 1896); *insight* (Sternberg and Davidson, 1985; Davidson 1992); *intuition* (Mackinnon, 1998; Myers and McCaulley 1985; Piirto & Johnson, 2004); *introversion* (Myers and McCaulley, 1985; Piirto & Johnson, 2004; Simonton, 1999a); *naiveté, or openness to experience* (Ghiselin, 1952; Cattell, 1971; Piirto, Montgomery, & Thurman, 2009); the presence of *overexcitabilities,* called OEs (Dabrowski, 1967; Piechowski 1979,

2006; Piirto, Montgomery, & May, 2008; Silverman, 1993); *perceptiveness* (Myers and McCaulley 1985); *perfectionism* (Piirto, Montgomery, & Thurman, 2008; Silverman, 1993, in press); *persistence* (Rayneri, Gerber, & Wiley, 2003; Renzulli, 1978); *preference for complexity* (Barron, 1968b, 1995; Mackinnon, 1978); *resilience* (Jenkins-Friedman, 1992; Block & Kremen, 1996); *risk-taking* (MacKinnon, 1978; Torrance, 1987); *self-discipline* (Renzulli, 1978); *self-efficacy* (Zimmerman, Bandura, and Martinez-Pons, 1992; Sternberg and Lubart 1992); *tolerance for ambiguity* (Barron, 1968b; 1995); and *volition, or will.* (Corno and Kanfer, 1993; Simonton, 1999a). The consolidation of personality traits into the Big Five (McCrae & Costa, 1999) is noted here, but earlier work on creative people has noted these other traits as listed, and so I include them here. Creative adults who achieve success possess many of these attributes.

[26] Intensity is the common word for the psychological term "overexcitability," based on the Dabrowski theory of emotional development—where it is theorized that creators who reach the highest levels of development have intensities – intellectual, emotional, imaginational, sensual, and psychomotor, with intellectual, emotional, and imaginational being absolutely necessary.

[27] Numerous studies have come from the Institute for Personality Assessment and Research (IPAR). IPAR was formed after World War II at the University of California in Berkeley. MacKinnon (1978) directed this Institute, after serving with the Office of Special Services on its assessment staff. In 1949 the Rockefeller Foundation granted funds to start IPAR, with the purpose of determining which people were most highly effective, and what made them that way. Among the people studied were writers, architects, engineering students, women mathematicians, inventors, and research scientists. The Institute studied people who were chosen by peer nomination; that is, the nominators were college professors, professionals in the field, and respected experts or connoisseurs knowledgeable about the field. Among the researchers there were Frank Barron, Donald MacKinnon, Harrison Gough, Ravenna Helson, Donald Crutchfield, and Erik Erikson (Helson 1999).

At IPAR, Frank Barron and his colleagues asked professors for the names of the most creative of outstanding creators in literature, mathematics, architecture, science, and other fields (Barron, 1968a, b; 1969; 1972; 1995). They invited them to come to the University of California to partici-pate in extensive testing and interviewing, and these studies pioneered some of the tests and interview techniques still used in studying human personality attributes and characteristics, for example, the Q-sort method of interviewing and the Barron- Welsh Art Scale for evaluating works of art. The IPAR studies were seminal in the research on creators.

[28] Barron, 1968a.

[29] McCutchan, 1999, p. 72.

[30] See Ericsson, 1996.

[31] My 2002 book is called *"My Teeming Brain": Understanding Creative Writers*; (Piirto, 2002a) and before that I did a study of women creative writers (Piirto, 1998a). "My teeming brain" is a quote from the Keats sonnet. "When I have fears that I may cease to be / Before my pen has gleaned my teeming brain . . ."

[32] See Stein, 1998; Brown, 2001.

[33] Ericsson, 1996; Ericsson, Charness, Feltovich, & Hoffman (Eds.). (2006).

[34] Stevens & Swan, 2004.

[35] Van Gogh, 1935, p. 45.

[36] Kuh, p. 12.

[37] deMille, 1991, p. 124.

[38] McCutchan, p. 28.

[39] *Chalk* (2006), directed by Mike Akel, is an improvised fiction film depicting a high school and its teachers throughout one school year. Mr. Lowery, the new teacher, is portrayed by Troy Schwemmer.

[40] Many internet sites exist about enhancing self-discipline. These five suggestions came from this site: http://www.ryanwhiteside.com/learning-self-discipline.html

[41] Spender, 1999.

[42] Stravinsky, 1990, p. 11.
[43] Hirschfield, 1996, p. 38.
[44] Hirshfield, p. 38.
[45] Barron, 1968b; Mackinnon, 1978.
[46] May, 1975.
[47] Chency, 1981.
[48] Neel, 2007.
[49] Interview with Anne Sexton by B. Kevles, 1968, collected in Plimpton, 1989, p. 268.
[50] Allison, D. Cited in Graff, 1995, p. 42.
[51] Among useful sources are state guidance guidelines such as http://www.learnnc.org/lp/editions/firstyear/258
[52] Breslin, 1993.
[53] http://jig.joelpomerantz.com/otherwriters/ginsberg.html. See also Miles' biography of Ginsberg
[54] Keats' theory of "negative capability" was expressed in his letter to George and Thomas Keats dated Sunday, 22 December 1817.
[55] Simon, 2003. (cf. Adorno, Frenkel-Brunswik, Levinson, & Sanford, 1950) (Cited by http://www.roadtopeace.org/index.php?itemid=86, ¶ 16).
[56] Bird and Sherman, 2005.
[57] Isaacson, 2007, location 536, Kindle.
[58] See the Creative Probem Solving Toolbox. See Treffinger, et al.
[59] Sawyer, 2007.
[60] Koepp, 2002, p. 14.
[61] Keynote speech by Henry Tirsi, research director of Nokia, US, September, 2004, European Council for High Ability Conference, Pamplona, Spain.
[62] Spender, 1998, p. 159.
[63] Hoffman, 1998.
[64] McCutchan, p. 36.
[65] This exercise is from my friend, F. Christopher Reynolds, who often teaches creativity as an adjunct professor, and who gives workshops with me. See Reynolds, 1990, for the creativity course he offers, called Creativity, Inc.
[66] from F. Christopher Reynolds. Various.
[67] This novel was published in 1985, and was the winner, over 75 other entries, of the Carpenter Press Tenth Anniversary First Novel Contest.
[68] These were modified from http://wilderdom.com/group/SocialSupportWaysToPromote.html. There are many such available in the literature and on the internet. Choose what seems to work in your classroom.
[69] Plato, Ion, The Banquet, The Meno, Phaedo, Phaedrus.
[70] In Berg (1983), p. 13.
[71] Sessions, p. 38.
[72] Personal communication, Laura WoodsThe entry continued, "I wonder if the worksheet queen at our school has felt the charge of creativity—or has it been so long that she doesn't crave it any longer?"
[73] Szymborska, 1997, p. 6.
[74] Maritain, 1953, p. 91.
[75] Maritain, 1953; Plato, Dialogues.
[76] Two for the road. Newsweek, July 27, 1998, p. 56.
[77] Waldman, in Johnson & Paulenich (Eds.), p. 315.
[78] McCutchan, 1999, p. 121.
[79] Johnson, 2006, Kindle location 1756.
[80] Pareles, 1997. Npg [web]
[81] Rhodes, 2004.
[82] Tesla, 2007, mark 227, Kindle.

NOTES

[83]   Isaacson, 2007, mark 499, Kindle.
[84]   Michaelis, 1998, p. 181.
[85]   Michaelis, p. 333.
[86]   See my poem, "Spring Beauties," on my website: http://web.me.com/janepiirto/Jane_Piirto_site/ Spring_Beauties.html
[87]   Many of these ideas are from my colleague's book (Broda, 2007).
[88]   Gardner added this intelligence to his basic 7 in the late 1990s. See Gardner, 1983, 1995, 1999. Naturalist intelligence is the intelligence that emphasizes classification and agriculture. Gardner does not add an intelligence to his theoretical framework unless it meets his 8 criteria for the presence of a frame of mind, including that it has an evolutionary basis in humankind.
[89]   Boehme was a German Lutheran mystic theologian whose book, *Aurore*, never completed, was an inspiration to writers.
[90]   Ribot, p. 336.
[91]   *Contemporary Authors Autobiography series, 11, (CAA)* p. 4.
[92]   Moyers, 1995, p. 383.
[93]   Blake, letter to Thomas Butts, April 25, 1803. http://www.wwnorton.com/college/English/naellnoa/ pdf/27636_Roma_U22_Poetry.pdf
[94]   Interview with Sam Waterston. In Robert Knopf, p. 365.
[95]   May, 1998, p. 112.
[96]   Abell, 1955. Kindle position 120ff.
[97]   Lucier, 1999, p. 46.
[98]   This film, from director Julien Temple in 2000, also shows the image of William Wordsworth and his faithful sister, Dorothy, tramping the hills and writing poems. See the General Practice for the Creative Process of walking.
[99]   "Rehab." Amy Winehouse, winner of 5 Grammy awards, including Record of the Year and Song of the Year, 2008. See Knafo, 2008.
[100] Baracka , the former Leroi Jones, is a controversial figure. He was slated to become Poet Laureate of the state of New Jersey when he wrote that the 9/11 tragedy was an Israeli government plot. Governor McGreevy tried to depose him, but finding there was no legal way to do so, he abolished the Poet Laureate position.
[101] These experiments are detailed in Robert Greenfield's 2006 biography of Timothy Leary.
[102] Barron , 1963, p. 247. See also de Rios & Janiger, 2003; Kerr, et al., 1991; Krippner, 1977; Leonard, 1989.
[103] Poincaré, p. 25.
[104] Saintsbury, pp. viii.
[105] McCutchan, p. 126.
[106] Robert Olen Butler, Personal communication, Baylor University, Art & Soul Conference, Waco, TX, February 2003.
[107] Tolson & Cuyjet, 2008.
[108] Ritz, location 640, Kindle.
[109] http://www.vh1.com/shows/dyn/celebrity_rehab_with_dr_drew/series.jhtml
[110] Greenfield, 2006, p. 174.
[111] Oral history interview with Romare Bearden, 1968 June 29, Archives of American Art, Smithsonian Institution. Interview with Romare Bearden conducted by Henri Ghent.
[112] Harris, 1964.
[113] Chilvers, 1990.
[114] Murray, 1984, 2003.
[115] Carr, 1971; Crean, 2001; Walker, 1990.
[116] Bird & Sherwin, 2005, p. 222.
[117] McCutchan, 1999, p. 49.
[118] Csikzentmihalyi, 1995.

[119] *The Journey*, the book that inspired Springsteen, was written by Dale Maharidge and the photos were by Michael Williamson. See Heyboer, 1996.

[120] Rogers, p. 40.

[121] Perhaps you could call me a museum collector. Among others, I've seen the museums of Paris, Moscow, Rome, Vienna, Budapest, Prague, London, Helsinki, Amsterdam, Madrid, Barcelona, Bilbao, Athens, Peking, Shanghai, Adelaide, Christchurch, Melbourne, Naples, New York, Boston, Los Angeles, San Francisco, Chicago, Denver, and on and on. One year I visited the Chagall and Matisse museums in Nice, and the museum of Timber Lake, South Dakota, on the edge of the Sioux Reservation, where the community was not even a hundred years old, and where the museum houses tribal, farming, and ethnic artifacts from the tribes and the settlers, and had one of the best museum shops with authentic Sioux art works. All of these have inspired creative works. A fine book on little museums is called just that, by Arany and Hobson (1998).

[122] Hoffman, 1998.

[123] Kuh, p. 219.

[124] Kurosawa, 1990.

[125] See Schredl & Erlacher, 2007.

[126] See 2006.

[127] http://www.achievement.org/autodoc/page/geh0int-2

[128] Aizenstat (2004), Hollis (), Reed (1988, Roomy (1990) are some of the depth psychologists whose dream work has affected me. I took workshops from Aizenstat and Reed. The exercise is a combination of several depth psychological approaches-Jung's active imagination is the impetus.

[129] Amplification is a term used by Jung and in art therapy. Amplification is of two types: subjective and objective. Subjective amplification uses "active imagination," a technique whereby the creator makes mental or art-based images to emerge while meditating or observing. Objective amplification illuminates the image or symbol through historical or mythological illustrations (Malchiodi, 2003).

[130] McCutchan, p. 5.

[131] Hale, 1987, p. 236. Hale commented: "this relentless experience, these passionate symbols, struck home with the impact of the elemental. She was helpless—not so much against Egypt, as against her own instinctive recognition of it."

[132] Poincaré, p. 26.

[133] Amodeo, p. 130.

[134] Piirto & Reynolds, 2007. *Journeys to Sacred Places; Places Sacred.* This is a chapbook of poems I have written while traveling to sacred places. My friend Christopher Reynolds added a CD of his songs, keyed to the poems.

[135] Bowman-Kruhm, 2003, p. 97.

[136] See Mujica, p. 36.

[137] Abra, 1995.

[138] *A Cemetery Special.* Rick Sebak, Producer and Narrator PBS Documentary. Aired October 31, 2005.

[139] *Brace for Impact: The Chester B. Sullenberger Story*, The Learning Channel documentary, January 10, 2010.

[140] I've written articles about synchronicity for the *Encyclopedia of Creativity*, editions 1 (Piirto, 1999d) and 2 (Piirto, 2011 in press). Synchronicity is rife in creativity—the fortuitous coincidence that is not a coincidence.

[141] Location 2421, Kindle.

[142] Cited in Abra, 1995, p. 208.

[143] The long-lasting rivalry between Helena Rubenstein and Elizabeth Arden was described in *The Powder and the Glory.* PBS documentary. March 23, 2009.

[144] Turner, 1985.

[145] Suggested by Lancaster PA: *366 community service ideas for students*: http://lancaster.unl.edu/4h/serviceideas.shtml

[146] Houtz & Patricola, 1999.

[147] Einstein, in Isaacson, Kindle location 750.

[148] http://www.achievement.org/autodoc/page/lin0int-6

[149] Murphy & Martin, 2002.

[150] From the seminal book on classroom imagery Bagley and Hess, 1983.

[151] Sartre, 1940.

[152] Chency, 1981, p. 12.

[153] Stanislavski, first edition published in 1936, reprinted in 1964, p. 54.

[154] Stanislavski, p. 71.

[155] See Strograz, "Finding Your Roots," http://opinionator.blogs.nytimes.com/2010/03/07/finding-your-roots/?em

[156] Bunge, 1962.

[157] Hoffman, 1998.

[158] Barron, 1968; Mackinnon, 1985; Myers & McCaulley, 1985.

[159] p. 401.

[160] Gladwell is an eloquent synthesizer and populizer of contemporary psychological thought. http://www.gladwell.com/blink/index.html

[161] Cappon, 1994, pp. 15–16.

[162] Kuh, p. 66.

[163] Bache, pp. 22–23.

[164] Franck, 1983.

[165] See Wallas, 1926.

[166] See Navarre, 1979; Smith & Dodds, 1999.

[167] See Segal, 2004.

[168] See Wells, 1996.

[169] Mullis, 1997.

[170] newsletter@americanpublicmedia.org, March 7, 2009. *The Writer's Almanac.*

[171] Gruber, 1996, interview with Piaget, 1969, p. 134.

[172] Sawyer (2006) called them "mini-insights," a result of the "hard conscious work that preceded them" (p. 71).

[173] Bird & Sherwin, 2005.

[174] See Kuh, 1990, p. 131.

[175] See Fay, 2000.

[176] http://www.achievement.org/autodoc/page/tha0int-3

[177] See Boal, 2002.

[178] Spolin, 1963.

[179] I recently wrote an encyclopedia entry for the *Encyclopedia of Creativity* about Ella Fitzgerald and her creativity in scat singing: Piirto, 2011. Scat singing is arguably what Fitzgerald is most famous for. She was able to improvise and range over two octaves, always perfectly in tune. Her recording of George Gershwin's "Oh, Lady Be Good" in 1947 is a classic of her scat style.

[180] Roth, 1992.

[181] Storr, 1988.

[182] Hosmer, 1993, p. 80.

[183] Buber, 1985, p. 11.

[184] McCutchan, 1999, p. 48.

[185] Dubos, 1950, p. 60.

[186] Spender, p. 83.

[187] Personal communication, Finnfest speech, Northern Michigan University, August, 2000.

[188] Toni Morrison, The Art of Fiction No. 134, *Paris Review.* Interviewed by Claudia Brodsky Lacour and Elissa Schappell. http://www.theparisreview.org/interviews/1888/the-art-of-fiction-no-134-toni-morrison

[189] Alfaro, 2006.

[190] Tolstoy, in A. B. Goldenveizer's *Talks with Tolstoy* (1923), p. 67.

[191] Kuh, 1990, p. 116, p. 97.

[192] Johnson & Paulenich, 1991, p. 1.

[193] Loori, location 1880, Kindle.

[194] Sternberg & Lubart, 1999, p. 3.

[195] Interview on National Public Radio, January 16, 2009.

[196] Alfaro, p. 28.

[197] http://www.acmhe.org/

[198] See Gates, 2005, p. 149.

[199] Even such venerable and practical sources as the New York *Times* have written about classroom meditation: See Brown, 2007. http://www.nytimes.com/2007/06/16/us/16mindful.html
See Zinger, 2008 for an example of meditative practice in the college classroom.

[200] He continued: "give students problems to explore rather than tasks to complete. Many students are under the impression that any problem that cannot be finished in five minutes is probably unsolvable. We can counter this notion by giving students mathematics projects that take weeks to complete instead of minutes. I shall cite just two examples: a class of sixth graders spent two weeks researching number systems, inventing one of their own, and creating a project explaining how their invented system would affect some aspect of our daily lives–for example, what would a base-five system be like? In a first-year-algebra class, after looking at the "handshake problem"–how many handshakes would be exchanged in a room filled with twenty people–students worked on individual projects exploring number sequences. Some students investigated Fibonacci numbers, whereas others searched for formulas that would describe different sequences. One student discovered an equation that would find the sum of any sequence regardless of the distance between each number. Imagine the depth of understanding these students will have gained compared with those who finished a unit and passed the test in the same amount of time" (p. 6).

[201] See Erikson & Erikson, 1991, p. 116. Pound, 1992.

[202] In Hodges, 1992. [From James Boswell: *Life of Samuel Johnson,*L.L.D. (1791). Aetat.28. To Angela Burdett-Coutts, Nov. 12, 1842: *The Letters of Charles Dickens:* The Pilgrim Edition (1965–81), iii, p. 367. Pacing quote, p. 216.]

[203] Gildner has a poem called "The Runner." Irving's wrestling is well-known; he played a wrestling coach in one of the movies made from his novels.

[204] Ornstein (1995) would call them "high gainers," or "introverts," who have extremely high sensitivity to stimulation. The Dabrowski theorists may call them "overexcitable" and "sensitive."

[205] Hodges, 1992, p. 217.

[206] Interview, ABC Cleveland, March 28, 2009. http://www.newsnet5.com/video/19031877/index.html

[207] Dillard, 1988.

[208] e.g., Proctor, 1999.

[209] Florida (2003).

[210] Rogers, 1976; Maslow, 1968 Perls (Amendt-Lyon, 2001); Dyer, 2006.

[211] Moyers, 1982; Goleman, Kaufman & Ray, 1992.

[212] Cameron, 1990; Goldberg, 1986; Progoff, 1980; Edwards, 1979; Campbell, 1997; Roth, 1992.

[213] See Piirto, 1999c.

[214] Jung, 1992.

[215] Plato, Ion.

[216] From the *Salon* interview with Russell Banks by Cynthia Joyce, January, 1998. http://www.salon.com/books/int/1998/01/cov_si_05int2.html

[217] Stone, p. 410.

[218] Duncan, p. 206.

[219] Boyd, 1992, p. 91.

[220] Adapted from Sullivan, 1994.

[221] Here I paste and paraphrase myself from *Understanding Those Who Create* (1992; 1998) and Chapter 4 in *Understanding Creativity* (Piirto, 2004). I also published a chapter about this (Piirto, 2000).

[222] See Piirto, 2007a; 2009a.

NOTES

[223] See Andrew Neel documentary, *Alice Neel.*

[224] See Bryant and Zillman, 1989.

[225] "Norms" for meetings are recommended by the professional learning communities (PLC) movement. See Dufour and Eaker, 1998.
   Collaborative Teams in Professional Learning Communities at Work. Solution Tree, 2009.

[226] Jung, 1977.

[227] See Hillman, 1996; Jung, 1965.

REFERENCES

Abell, A. (1955). *Talks with great composers: Candid conversations with Brahms, Puccini, Strauss, and Others.* New York: Citadel.

Abra, J. (1995). Do the Muses dwell in Elysium? Death as a motive for creativity. *Creativity Research Journal, 8*(3), 215–228.

Adler, M. (1952). *The great ideas: A syntopticon of great books of the western world.* Chicago: The Encycopaedia Britannica.

Adorno, T., Frenkel-Brunwik, E., Levinson, D., & Sanford, N. (1950). *The authoritarian personality: Studies in prejudice series* (Vol. 1). New York: W. W. Norton.

Aizenstadt, S. (2004, August 25). *Dream tending: Techniques for uncovering the hidden intelligence of your dreams.* Workshop handout. Santa Barbara, CA: Pacifica Graduate Institute.

Akel, M. (Producer, Director). (2007). *Chalk.* Austin, TX: Someday Soon Productions.

Alfaro, N. (2006, November). Mind your body: Meditation how stillness improves performance skills. *Dance Magazine, 80*(11), 28–29.

Albert, R. S. (1975). Toward a behavioral definition of genius. *American Psychologist, 30,* 140–151.

Allen, J. S. (1992). Educating performers. *The American Scholar, 61*(2), 197–209.

Amabile, T. (1996). *Creativity in context.* Boulder, CO: Westfield Press.

Amendt-Lyon, N. (2001). Art and creativity in gestalt therapy. *The Gestalt Review, 5,* 225–248.

Amodeo, C. (2002). Q&A: Martin Cruz Smith. *Geographical, 74*(12), 130.

Arany, L., & Hobson, M. (1998). *Little (and not so little) museums.* New York: Henry Holt.

Artress, L. (1995). *Walking a sacred path: Rediscovering the labyrinth.* New York: Berkeley Publishing Group.

Bache, C. M. (2008). *The living classroom: Teaching and collective consciousness.* Albany, NY: State University of New York Press.

Baird, L. L. (1985). Do grades and tests predict adult accomplishment? *Research in Higher Education, 23*(1), 3–85.

Barron, F. X. (1963). *Creativity and psychological health: Origins of personal vitality and creative freedom.* Princeton, NJ: Van Nostrand.

Barron, F. X. (1968a). The dream of art and poetry. *Psychology Today, 2*(7), 18–23, 66.

Barron, F. X. (1968b). *Creativity and personal freedom.* New York: Van Nostrand.

Barron, F. X. (1972). *Artists in the making.* New York: Seminar Press.

Barron, F. X. (1995). *No rootless flower: An ecology of creativity.* Cresskill, NJ: Hampton Press.

Berg, S. (Ed.). (1983). *In praise of what persists.* New York: Harper & Row.

Bernardi, P. (1992). *Improvisation starters: A collection of 900 improvisation situations for the theater.* Cincinnati, OH: Betterway Books.

Berkman, R. M. (1995). Mathematics in the slow lane: Taking the scenic route. *Teaching Children Mathematics, 2,* 6 ff.

Bird, K., & Sherwin, M. J. (2005). *American Prometheus: The triumph and tragedy of J. Robert Oppenheimer.* New York: Vintage Books.

Boal, A. (2002). *Games for actors and non-actors.* London: Routledge.

Bowman-Kruhm, M. (2003). *Margaret Mead: A biography.* Westport, CT: Greenwood Press.

Boyd, J. (1992). *Musicians in tune.* New York: Simon and Schuster, Inc.

Breslin, J. E. B. (1993). *Mark Rothko: A biography.* Chicago: University of Chicago Press.

Broda, H. W. (2007). *Schoolyard-enhanced learning: Using the outdoors as an instructional tool, K-8.* Portland, ME: Stenhouse Publishers.

Brown, M. H. (2001). A psychosynthesis twelve step program for transforming consciousness: Creative explorations of inner space. *Counseling and Values, 45*(2), 103–110.

Brown, P. L. (2007, June 16). In the classroom, a new focus on quieting the mind. *New York Times.* Retrieved January 15, 2010, from http://www.nytimes.com/2007/06/16/us/16mindful.html

REFERENCES

Bryant, J., & Zillman, D. (1989). Using humor to promote learning in the classroom. In P. McGhee (Ed.), *Humor and children's development* (pp. 49–78). Binghamton, NY: Haworth Press.

Buber, M. (1985). *Ecstatic confessions* (P. Mendes-Flohr, Trans.). New York: Harper & Row. (Original published in German *as Ekstatische Konvessionen*, 1909)

Bunge, M. (1962). *Intuition and science*. Englewood Cliffs, NJ: Prentice-Hall.

Calame, C. (1995). *The craft of poetic speech in ancient Greece* (J. Orion, Trans.). Ithaca, NY: Cornell University Press.

Callahan, M. (1997). Creation myth. In F. Barron, A. Montuori, & A. Barron (Eds.), *Creators on creating* (pp. 216–221). Los Angeles: Jeremy T. Tarcher/Putnam.

Cameron, J. (1992). *The artist's way: A spiritual path to higher creativity*. Los Angeles: Jeremy Tarcher.

Campbell, D. (1997). *The Mozart effect: Tapping the power of music to heal the body, strengthen the mind, and unlock the creative spirit*. New York: Avon.

Cappon, D. (1994). *Intuition and management: Research and application*. Westport, CT: Quorum Books.

Carr, E. (1971). *Klee Wyck*. Toronto: Clark Irwin.

Cattell, J. M. (1903). A statistical study of eminent men. *Popular Science Monthly, 62*, 359–377.

Cattell, R. B. (1971). *Abilities: Their structure, growth, and action*. Boston: Houghton Mifflin Co.

Cattell, R. B. (1990). Advances in Cattellian personality psychology. In H. Pervin (Ed.), *Handbook of personality: Theory and research* (pp. 101–111). New York: Guilford Press.

Chency, M. (1981). *Tesla: Man of our time*. New York: Barnes & Noble Books.

Chilvers, I. (Ed.). (1990). *The concise Oxford dictionary of art and artists*. Oxford: Oxford University Press.

Clapton, E. (2007). *Clapton, the autobiography*. New York: Broadway Books.

Corno, L., & Kanfer, R. (1993). The role of volition in learning and performance. In L. Darling-Hammond (Ed.), *Review of research in education* (Vol. 19, pp. 301–342). Washington, DC: American Educational Research Association.

Costa, P. T., Jr., & McCrae, R. R. (1992). *NEO PI-R professional manual*. Odessa, FL: Psychological Assessment Resources, Inc.

Crean, S. (2001). *The laughing one: A journey to Emily Carr*. Toronto: Harpercollins Canada.

Csikszentmihalyi, M. (1990). *Flow: The psychology of optimal experience*. New York: Cambridge.

Csikszentmihalyi, M. (1995). *Creativity*. New York: Harpercollins.

Csikszentmihalyi, M., Rathunde, K., & Whalen, S. (1993). *Talented teenagers: The roots of success and failure*. New York: Cambridge University Press.

Dabrowski, K. (1967). *Personality-shaping through positive disintegration*. Boston: Little, Brown.

Davidson, J. E. (1992). Insights about giftedness: The role of problem solving abilities. In N. Colangelo, S. G. Assouline, & D. L. Ambroson (Eds.), *Talent development: Proceedings from the 1991 Henry B. and Jocelyn Wallace national research symposium on talent development* (pp. 125–142). Unionville, NY: Trillium Press.

deMille, A. (1991). *Martha: The life and work of Martha Graham*. New York: Random House.

De Rios, M. D., & Janiger, O. (2003). *LSD, spirituality, and the creative process*. Rochester, VT: Park Street Press.

Dubos, R. J. (1950). *Louis Pasteur, free lance of science*. Boston: Little, Brown.

Dufour, R., & Eaker, R. (1998). *Professional learning communities at work: Best practices for enhancing student achievement*. Bloomington, IN: National Educational Service.

Duncan, I. (1997). The mother of creation. In F. Barron, A. Montuori, & A. Barron (Eds.), *Creators on creating* (pp. 196–207). Los Angeles: Jeremy Tarcher.

Dyer, W. (2006). *Inspiration: Your ultimate calling*. Carlsbad, CA: Hay House.

Eberle, B. (1996). *Scamper*. Waco, TX: Prufrock Press.

Edwards, B. (1979). *Drawing on the right side of the brain*. Los Angeles: Tarcher.

Ericsson, K. A. (1996). *The road to excellence: The acquisition of expert performance in the arts and sciences, sports, and games*. Mahwah, NJ: Erlbaum.

Ericsson, K. A., Charness, N., Feltovich, P., & Hoffman, R. R. (Eds.). (2006). *Cambridge handbook on expertise and expert performance*. Cambridge, UK: Cambridge University Press.

Erikson, E., & Erikson, J. (1991). Lifework. *Re-vision, 14*(2), 114–118.

Eysenck, H. J. (1993). Creativity and personality: Suggestions for a theory. *Psychological Inquiry, 4*(3), 147–178.

Fay, L. E. (2000). *Shostakovich: A life*. New York: Oxford University Press.

Florida, R. (2003). *Rise of the creative class*. New York: Basic Books.

Franck, F. (1983). *The Zen of seeing: Drawing as meditation*. New York: Random House.

Freud, S. (1908/1976). Creative writers and daydreaming. In A. Rothenberg & C. Hausman (Eds.), *The creativity question* (pp. 48–52). Durham, NC: Duke University Press. (Original work published 1908)

Gardner, H. (1983). *Frames of mind*. New York: Basic.

Gardner, H. (1993). *Creating minds*. New York: Basic Books.

Gardner, H. (1999). *Intelligence reframed: Multiple intelligences for the 21st Century*. New York: Basic Books.

Gardner, J. (1978). *On moral fiction*. New York: Basic Books.

Gates, G. (2005). Awakening to school community: Buddhist philosophy for educational reform. *The Journal of Educational Thought, 39*, 149–156.

Ghiselin, B. (Ed.). (1952). *The creative process*. New York: Mentor.

Gladwell, M. (2005). *Blink: The power of thinking without thinking*. New York: Little, Brown, and Company.

Goldberg, N. (1986). *Writing down the bones*. New York: Quality Paperbacks.

Goleman, D., Kaufman, P., & Ray, M. (1992). *The creative spirit*. New York: Dutton.

Gopnik, B. (2008, December 16). Masters & commander. Paris's "Picasso" captures cubist's inspirations and variations, from precursors. *Washington Post*, p. C01.

Gough, H. G. (1979). A creative personality scale for the adjective check list. *Journal of Personality and Social Psychology, 37*, 1398–1405.

Graff, E. J. (1995). Novelist out of Carolina. *Poets & Writers Magazine, 23*(1), 40–49.

Greenfield, R. (2006). *Timothy Leary: A biography*. New York: Harcourt Books.

Gruber, H. E. (1996). The life space of a scientist: The visionary function and other aspects of Jean Piaget's thinking. *Creativity Research Journal, 9*, 251–266.

Guilford, J. P. (1950). Creativity. *American Psychologist, 5*, 444–454.

Guilford, J. P. (1967). *The nature of human intelligence*. New York: McGraw-Hill.

Hale, N. (1987). *Mary Cassatt*. New York: Doubleday.

Harris, L. (1964). *The story of the group of seven*. Toronto: Rous & Mann Press Limited.

Heyboer, K. (1996). Providing inspiration for the Boss. *American Journalism Review, 18*, 12.

Hillman, J. (1975). *Re-visioning psychology*. New York: HarperColophon Books.

Hillman, J. (1996). *The soul's code: In search of character and calling*. New York: Random House.

Hirshfield, J. (1996). Komachi on the stoop: Writing and the threshold life. *American Poetry Review, 25*, 29–38.

Hodges, J. (1992). *The genius of writers: A treasury of facts, anecdotes, and comparisons: The lives of English writers compared*. New York: St. Martin's Press.

Hoffman, P. (1998). *The man who loved only numbers: The story of Paul Erdös and the search for mathematical truth*. New York: Hyperion.

Hogan, L. (2001). *The woman who watches over the world: A native memoir*. New York: W.W. Norton.

Hollis, J. (2002). *The archetypal imagination*. College Station, TX: Texas A & M Press.

Hosmer, R. E. (1993). The art of poetry: Interview with Amy Clampitt. *The Paris Review, 126*, 76–109.

Houtz, J. C., & Patricola, C. (1999). Imagery. In M. Runco & S. Pritzker (Eds.), *The encyclopedia of creativity* (Vol. II, pp. 1–11). San Diego, CA: Academic Press.

Isaacson, W. (2007). *Einstein*. New York: Simon and Schuster.

Jenkins-Friedman, R. (1992). Zorba's conundrum: Evaluative aspect of self-concept in talented individuals. *Quest, 3*(1), 1–7.

Johnson, K. & Paulenich, C. (Eds.). (1991). *Beneath a single moon: Buddhism in contemporary American poetry*. Boston: Shambhala.

Johnson, P. W. (2006). *Creators: From Chaucer to Walt Disney*. New York: HarperCollins.

Jung, C. G. (1933). *Modern man in search of a soul*. New York: Bantam.

Jung, C. G. (1965). *Memories, dreams, reflections*. New York: Vintage.

Jung, C. G. (1971). *Psychological types* (R. F. C. Hull, Trans.). Bollingen Series XX. Princeton, NJ: Princeton University Press.

REFERENCES

Jung, C. (1972). *Mandala symbolism* (R. F. C. Hull, Trans.). Bollingen Series XXI. Princeton, NJ: Princeton University Press.

Jung, C. G. (1976). On the relation of analytical psychology to poetic art. In A. Rothenberg & C. Hausman (Eds.), *The creativity question* (pp. 120–126.) Durham, NC: Duke University Press. (Original work published 1923)

Kaufman, J. C. (2001). The Sylvia Plath effect: Mental illness in eminent creative writers. *Journal of Creative Behavior, 35*, 37–50.

Kaufman, J., & Baer, J. (Eds.). (2004). *Creativity in domains: Faces of the muse.* Parsippany, NJ: Lawrence Erlbaum.

Kerr, G., Shaffer, J., Chambers, C., & Hallowell, K. (1991). Substance use of creatively talented adults. *Journal of Creative Behavior, 25*, 145–153.

Kevles, B. (1968). Interview with Anne Sexton. In G. Plimpton (Ed.), (1989). *Women writers at work: The Paris review interviews* (pp. 263–290). New York: Viking.

Koepp, R. (2002). *Clusters of creativity: Enduring lessons on innovation and entrepreneurship from Silicon Valley and Europe's Silicon Fen.* New York: John Wiley & Sons.

Kogan, J. (1987). *Nothing but the best: The struggle for perfection at the Juilliard School.* New York: Random House.

Knafo, D. (2008). The senses grow skilled in their craving: Thoughts on creativity and addiction. *Psycho-analytic Review, 95*, 571–595.

Knopf, R. (Ed.). (2005). *Theater and film: A comparative anthology.* New Haven, CT: Yale University Press.

Krippner, S. (1977). Research in creativity and psychedelic drugs. *International Journal of Clinical and Experimental Hypnosis, 25*, 274–290.

Kuh, K. (1990). *The artist's voice: Talks with seventeen modern artists.* Cambridge, MA: DaCapo Press.

Kurosawa, A. (Director & Writer). (1990). *Dreams* [Motion picture]. United States: Warner Bros.

Leonard, L. S. (1989). *Witness to the fire: Creativity and the veil of addiction.* Boston: Shambhala.

Loori, J. D. (2005). *The Zen of creativity.* New York: Ballantine.

Lucier, J. (1999, March 29). Henri Matisse builds a chapel. *Insight on the News.*

MacKinnon, D. (1975). IPAR's contribution to the conceptualization and study of creativity. In I. A. Taylor & J. W. Getzels (Eds.), *Perspectives in creativity* (pp. 60–89). Chicago: Aldine Publishing Company.

MacKinnon, D. (1978). *In search of human effectiveness: Identifying and developing creativity.* Buffalo, NY: Bearly Limited.

Malchiodi, C. A. (2003). Psychoanalytic, analytic, and object relations approaches. In C. A. Machiodi (Ed.), *Handbook of art therapy* (pp. 41–57). New York: The Guilford Press.

Maslow, A. (1968). *Creativity in self-actualizing people. Toward a psychology of being.* New York: Van Nostrand Reinhold Company.

Maritain, J. (1953). *Creative intuition in art and poetry.* Trustees of the National Gallery of Art, Washington, DC. The A.W. Mellon Lectures in the Fine Arts. Bollingen series XXXV. Princeton, NJ: Princeton University Press.

Massey, I. J. (2006). The musical dream revisited: Music and language in dreams. *Psychology of aesthetics, creativity and the arts, 5*(1), 52–50.

May, R. (1975). *The courage to create.* New York: Bantam.

May, S. (1998, July). Rothko: Emotion in the abstract. *World and I, 13*(7), 110–113.

McCrae, R. R., & Costa, P. T. (1999). A five-factor theory of personality. In L. A. Pervin & O. P. John (Eds.), *Handbook of personality theory and research* (2nd ed., pp. 139–153). San Diego, CA: Academic Press.

McCutchan, A. (1999). *The muse that sings: Composers sing about the creative process.* New York: Oxford University Press.

Meeker, M. (1977). *The structure of intellect.* Columbus, OH: Merrill.

Michaelis, D. (1998). *N. C. Wyeth: A biography.* New York: HarperCollins Perennial.

Miles, B. (1989). *Ginsberg.* New York: Simon and Schuster.

Moyers, B. (1982). *Creativity.* Television series. Public Broadcasting Service.

Moyers, B. (1995). *The language of life: A festival of poets.* New York: Doubleday.

Mullis, K. (1997). The screwdriver. In F. Barron, A. Montuori, & A. Barron (Eds.), *Creators on creating* (pp. 68–73). Los Angeles: Jeremy P. Tarcher/Putnam.

Murray, J. (1984). *The best of the group of seven.* Toronto: McClelland and Stewart, Ltd.

Murray, J. (2003). *Lawren Harris: An introduction to his life and art.* Toronto: Firefly Books.

Murphy, S. M., & Martin, K. A. (2002). The use of imagery in sport. In T. S. Horn (Ed.), *Advances in sport psychology* (2nd ed., pp. 405–439). Champaign, IL: Human Kinetics.

Myers, I. B, & McCaulley, M. H. (1985). *Manual: A guide to the development and use of the Myers-Briggs type indicator.* Palo Alto, CA: Consulting Psychologists Press.

Navarre, J. P. (1979). Incubation as fostering the creative process. *Gifted Child Quarterly, 23,* 792–800.

Neel, A. (Producer). (2007). *Alice Neel: A documentary.* New York: SeeThink Productions. Documentary film.

Newton, B. (1998). *Improvisation: Use what you know—make up what you don't.* Scottsdale, AZ: Great Potential Press.

Ornstein, R. (1995). *The roots of the self.* New York: Harpercollins.

Osborn, A. (1953). *Applied imagination.* New York: Scribner's.

Palmer, P. J. (2007). *The courage to teach: Exploring the inner landscape of a teacher's life.* San Francisco: Jossey-Bass.

Perkins, D. (1981). *The mind's best work.* Boston: Harvard University Press.

Piechowski, M. M. (1979). Developmental potential. In N. Colangelo & R. T. Zaffrann (Eds.), *New voices in counseling the gifted* (pp. 25–57). Dubuque, IA: Kendall/Hunt.

Piechowski, M. M. (2006). *"Mellow Out," they say: If only I could".* Madison, WI: Yunasa Press.

Piirto, J. (1985). *The three-week trance diet.* Columbus, OH: Carpenter Press.

Piirto, J. (1992). *Understanding those who create.* Dayton, OH: Ohio Psychology Press.

Piirto, J. (1994). *Talented children and adults: Their development and education.* New York: Macmillan.

Piirto, J. (1995a). Deeper and broader: The pyramid of talent development in the context of the giftedness construct. In M. W. Katzko & F. J. Mönks (Eds.), *Nurturing talent: Individual needs and social ability* (pp. 10–20). Proceedings of the Fourth Conference of the European Council for High Ability. The Netherlands: Van Gorcum, Assen.

Piirto, J. (1995b). Deeper and broader: The pyramid of talent development in the context of the giftedness construct. *Educational Forum, 59,* 364–369.

Piirto, J. (1998a.) Themes in the lives of contemporary U.S. women creative writers at midlife. *Roeper Review, 21*(1), 60–70.

Piirto, J. (1998b). *Understanding those who create* (2nd ed.). Scottsdale, AZ: Gifted Psychology Press.

Piirto, J. (1999a). *Talented children and adults: Their development and education* (2nd ed.). Columbus, OH: Prentice Hall/Merrill.

Piirto, J. (1999b). A different approach to creativity enhancement. *Tempo, XIX,* 3, 1, ff.

Piirto, J. (1999c). Metaphor and image in counseling the talented. *Spotlight: Newsletter of the Arts Division of the National Association for Gifted Children,* 6–7.

Piirto, J. (1999d). Synchronicity. In M. Runco & S. Pritzker (Eds.), *Encyclopedia of creativity* (Vol. 2, pp. 591–596). San Diego, CA: Academic Press.

Piirto, J. (2000). How parents and teachers can enhance creativity in children. In M. D. Gold & C. R. Harris (Eds.), *Fostering creativity in children, K-8: Theory and practice* (pp. 49–68). Needham Heights, MA: Allyn & Bacon.

Piirto, J. (2001). The Piirto pyramid of talent development: A conceptual framework. *Gifted Children Today, 23*(6), 22–29.

Piirto, J. (2002a). *"My teeming brain": Understanding creative writers.* Cresskill, NJ: Hampton Press.

Piirto, J. (2002b). The question of quality and qualifications: Writing inferior poems as qualitative research. *International Journal of Qualitative Studies in Education, 15*(4), 431–445.

Piirto, J. (2002c). The unreliable narrator, or the difference between writing prose in literature and in social science. *International Journal of Qualitative Studies in Education, 15*(4), 407–415.

Piirto, J. (2004). *Understanding creativity.* Scottsdale, AZ: Great Potential Press.

Piirto, J. (2005a). The creative process in poets. In J. Kaufman & J. Baer (Eds.), *Creativity in domains: Faces of the muse* (pp. 1–21). Mahwah, NJ: Lawrence Erlbaum.

REFERENCES

Piirto, J. (2005b). Rethinking the creativity curriculum. *Gifted Education Communicator, 36*(2), 12–19. Journal of the California Association for the Gifted.

Piirto, J. (2007a). *Talented children and adults: Their development and education* (3rd ed.). Waco, TX: Prufrock Press.

Piirto, J. (2007b). Understanding visual artists and creative writers. In K. Tirri (Ed.), *Values and foundations in gifted education* (pp. 34–48). Pieterlen, Switzerland: Peter Lang International.

Piirto, J. (2007c). A postmodern view of the creative process. In J. Kincheloe & R. Horn (Eds.), *Educational psychology handbook*. Greenwood Press.

Piirto, J. (2008a). Understanding creativity in domains using the Piirto pyramid of talent development as a framework. *Mensa Research Journal, 39*(1), 74–84.

Piirto, J. (2008b). Giftedness in nonacademic domains. In S. Pfeiffer (Ed.), *Handbook of giftedness in children: Psych-educational theory, research, and best practices* (pp. 367–386). New York: Springer.

Piirto, J. (2008c). Rethinking the creativity curriculum: An organic approach to creativity enhancement. *Mensa Research Journal, 39*(1), 85–94.

Piirto, J. (2008f). Rethinking the creativity curriculum: An organic approach to creativity enhancement. *Mensa Research Journal, 39*(1), 85–94.

Piirto, J. (2008g). *Saunas: Poetry by Jane Piirto*. Bay City, MI: Mayapple Press.

Piirto, J. (2009a). Eminence and creativity in selected visual artists. In (Eds.), *Leading change in gifted education: The Festschrift of Dr. Joyce VanTassel-Baska* (pp. 13–26). Waco, TX: Prufrock Press.

Piirto, J. (2009b). Personalities of creative writers. In S. Kaufman & J. Kaufman (Eds.), *Psychology of creative writing*. New York: Cambridge University Press.

Piirto, J. (2009c). Eminent women. In B. Kerr (Ed.), *Encyclopedia of giftedness, creativity, and talent*. Academic Press.

Piirto, J. (2009d). The creative process as creators practice it: A view of creativity with emphasis on what creators really do. In B. Cramond, N. L. Hafenstein, & K. Haines (Eds.), *Perspectives in gifted education: Creativity monograph* (pp. 42–68). Denver, CO: University of Denver.

Piirto, J. (2010a). The five core attitudes and seven I's of creativity. In J. Kaufman & R. Beghetto (Eds.), *Nurturing creativity in the classroom* (pp. 142–171). New York: Cambridge.

Piirto, J. (in press, 2011a). Entry, synchronicity. In M. Runco & S. Pritzker (Eds.), *Encyclopedia of creativity* (2nd ed.). London: Elsevier Publications.

Piirto, J. (in press, 2011b). Themes in the lives of creative writers. In E. Grigorenko, E. Mambrino, & D. Preiss (Eds.), *Handbook of writing*. New York: Psychology Press.

Piirto, J., & Fraas, J. (1995). Androgyny in the personalities of talented adolescents. *Journal for Secondary Gifted Education, I,* 93–102.

Piirto, J., & Johnson, G. (2004). *Personality attributes of talented adolescents.* Paper presented at the National Association for Gifted Children conference, Salt Lake City, UT; at the Wallace Research Symposium, in Iowa City, IA; and at the European Council for High Ability conference, Pamplona, Spain.

Piirto, J., Montgomery, D., & May, J. (2008). A comparison of Ohio and Korean high school talented youth on the OEQ II. *High Ability Studies, 19,* 141–153.

Piirto, J., Montgomery, D., & Thurman, J. (2009, November 6). *Personality and perfectionism.* Study presented at National Association for Gifted Children meeting, St. Louis, MO.

Piirto, J., & Reynolds, F. C. (2007). *Journeys to sacred places: Places sacred: Poems and songs* (2nd ed.). Ashland, OH: Sisu Press.

Pink, D. (2006). *A whole new mind: Why right-brainers will rule the future*. New York: Riverhead Books.

Plato. (1929). *Five dialogues of Plato bearing on poetic inspiration* (P. B. Shelley, F. Syndenham, H. Cary, & J. Wright, Trans.). London: J. M. Dent.

Plato. (1952). The ion. In *Great books of the western world* (Vol. 7). Chicago: Encyclopedia Britannica.

Plato. (1954). The republic. In R. Ulrich (Ed.), *Three thousand years of educational wisdom: Selections from great documents* (P. Shorey, Trans., pp. 31–62). Cambridge, MA: Harvard Univ. Press.

Plomin, R. (1997). Genetics and intelligence. In N. Colangelo & G. Davis (Eds.), *Handbook of gifted education* (2nd ed., pp. 67–74). Boston: Allyn and Bacon.

Poincaré, H. (1985). Mathematical creation. In B. Ghiselin (Ed.), *The creative process* (pp. 22–31). Berkeley, CA: The University of California Press. From Henri Poincaré. "La raisonnement mathématique" *Science et methode*. French publishers, Ernest Flammarion, 1908, Paris.

Pound, E. (1992). *Walking tour in Southern France: Ezra Pound among the Troubadours*. New York: New Directions.

Proctor, T. (1999). *Creative problem solving for managers*. London: Routledge.

Progoff, I. (1980). *The practice of process meditation: The intensive journal way to spiritual experience*. New York: Dialogue House Library.

Rayneri, L. J., Gerber, B. L., & Wiley, L. P. (2003). Gifted achievers and gifted underachievers: The impact of learning style preferences in the classroom. *Journal of Secondary Gifted Education, 14*(4), 197–204.

Reed, H. (1988). *Getting help from your dreams*. New York: Ballantine.

Renzulli, J. (1978). What makes giftedness? Re_examining a definition. *Phi Delta Kappan, 60*, 180–184, 261.

Renzulli, J., Smith, L. H., White, A. J., Callahan, C. M., & Hartman, R. K. (1997). *Scales for rating the behavioral characteristics of superior group members*. Mansfield Center, CT: Creative Learning Press.

Reynolds, F. C. (1990). Mentoring artistic adolescents through expressive therapy. *Clearing House, 64*, 83–86.

Reynolds, F. C. (1997, July 13). *Reifying creativity during the adolescent passage*. Paper presented at Ashland University Ohio Summer Honors Institute.

Reynolds, F. C., & Piirto J. (2005). Depth psychology and giftedness: Bringing soul to the field of talent development education. *Roeper Review, 27*, 164–171.

Reynolds, F. C., & Piirto, J. (2007). Honoring and suffering the Thorn: Marking, naming, and eldering: Depth psychology, II. *Roeper Review, 29*, 48–53.

Reynolds, F. C., & Piirto, J. (2009). Depth psychology and integrity. In D. Ambrose & T. Cross (Eds.), *Morality, ethics, and gifted minds* (pp. 195–206). New York: Springer Science.

Rhodes, R. (2004). *John James Audubon: The making of an American*. New York: Alfred A. Knopf.

Ribot, T. (1906). *Essay on the creative imagination* (A. H. N. Baron, Trans.). London: K. Paul, Trench, Trubner.

Riggs, T. (Ed.). (1996). *Contemporary poets* (6th ed.). New York: St. James Press.

Ritz, D. (1987). *Divided soul: The life of Marvin Gaye*. New York: DaCapo.

Rogers, C. (1976). Toward a theory of creativity. In A. Rothenberg & C. Hausman (Eds.), *The creativity question* (pp. 296–305). Durham, NC: Duke University Press.

Rogers, J. (2008, June 16). The lure of the beach: A new generation of US bands cites the Beach Boys as a huge inspiration. Why now? *New Statesman, 137*, 41–42.

Roeckelein, J. E. (2004). *Imagery in psychology: A reference guide*. Westport, CT: Praeger.

Roomy, D. (1990). *Inner work in the wounded and creative: The dream in the body*. London, UK: Arkana.

Roth, G. (1992). *The wave* [Videotape]. Boston: Shambhala.

Rothenberg, A. (1979). *The emerging goddess: The creative process in art, science, and other fields*. Chicago: University of Chicago Press.

Runco, M. A. (2006). Reasoning and personal creativity. In J. C. Kaufman & J. Baer (Eds.), *Creativity and reason in cognitive development* (pp. 99–116). New York: Cambridge.

Saintsbury, G. (1901). *The works of Honoré de Balzac* (Vol. I). Philadelphia: Avil Publixhing Company.

Santayana, G. (1896). *The sense of beauty: Being the outline of aesthetic theory*. New York: Dover Publications.

Sartre, J. P. (1940). *L'Imaginaire: Psychologie phénoménologique de l'imagination*. Paris: Gallimard.

Sawyer, K. (2007). *Group genius: The creative power of collaboration*. New York: Basic Books.

Schredl, M., & Erlacher, D. (2007). Self-reported effects of dreams on waking-life creativity: An empirical study. *Journal of Psychology: Interdisciplinary and Applied, 141*(1), 35–46.

Sebak, R. [Producer]. (2005). *A cemetery special*. Documentary film. PBS.

Segal, E. (2004). Incubation in insight problem solving. *Creativity Research Journal, 16*(1), 141–148.

Sessions, R. (1985). The composer and his message. In B. Ghiselin (Ed.), *The creative process* (pp. 36–40). Berkeley, CA: University of California Press.

REFERENCES

Silverman, L. K. (Ed.). (1993). *Counseling the gifted and talented*. Denver, CO: Love.

Simonton, D. K. (1984). *Genius, creativity and leadership: Historiometric inquiries*. Cambridge, MA: Harvard University Press.

Simonton, D. K. (1986). Biographical typicality, eminence and achievement styles. *Journal of Creative Behavior, 20*(1), 17–18.

Simonton, D. K. (1988). *Scientific genius*. Cambridge, MA: Harvard University Press.

Simonton, D. K. (1991). The child parents the adult: On getting genius from giftedness. In N. Colangelo, S. G. Assouline, & D. L. Ambroson (Eds.), *Talent development: Proceedings from the 1991 Henry and Jocelyn Wallace National Research Symposium on Talent Development* (pp. 278–297). Unionville, NY: Trillium.

Simonton, D. K. (1994). *Greatness: Who makes history and why*. New York: The Guilford Press.

Simonton, D. K. (1999). *Origins of genius: Darwinian perspectives on creativity*. New York: Oxford University Press.

Smith, S. M., & Dodds, R. A. (1999). Incubation. In M. Runco & S. Pritzker (Eds.), *Encyclopedia of creativity* (Vol. 2, pp. 39–43). San Diego, CA: Academic Press.

Spender, M. (1999). *From a high place: A life of Arshile Gorky*. Berkeley, CA: University of California Press.

Spolin, V. (1963). *Improvisation for the theater: A handbook of teaching and directing techniques*. Chicago: Northwestern University Press.

Stanislavski, C. (1964). *An actor prepares* (Vol. 1). New York: Routledge/Theater Arts Books.

Stein, M. (1998). *Transformation: Emergence of the self*. College Station, TX: Texas A&M University Press.

Sternberg, R. J., & Davidson, J. (Eds.). (1995). *The nature of insight*. Cambridge, MA: MIT Press.

Sternberg, R., & Lubart, T. I. (1991). An investment theory of creativity and its development. *Human Development, 34*, 1–31.

Sternberg, R., & Lubart, T. (1999). The concept of creativity: Prospects and paradigms. In R. Sternberg (Ed.), *Handbook of creativity* (pp. 3–15). London, UK: Oxford University Press.

Stevens, M., & Swan, A. (2004). *De Kooning: An American master*. New York: Alfred A. Knopf.

Stravinsky, I. (1990). On conductors and conducting. *Journal of the Conductors' Guild, 11*(1 & 2), 9–18.

Stone, I. (1937). *Dear Theo: The autobiography of Vincent Van Gogh*. New York: New American Library.

Storr, A. (1988). *Solitude: A return to the self*. New York: Free Press.

Subotnik, R. F., Kassan, L., Summers, E., & Wasser, A. (1993). *Genius revisited: High IQ children grown up*. Norwood, NJ: Ablex.

Sullivan, K. (2004). The art of your room: What your classroom says about you. *School Arts, 103*(10), 30.

Szymborzka, W. (1997). The 1996 Nobel Lecture. In S. Barańczak & C. Cavanagh (Trans.), *World Literature Today, 71*(1), 6.

Taylor, C. W. (1974). Multiple talent teaching. *Today's Education*, 71–74.

Temple, J. [Director]. (2000). *Pandaemonium*. London: British Broadcasting Corporation.

Tesla, N. (2007). (Original text published 1919). *My inventions: The autobiography of Nikola Tesla*. New York: Cosimo Books.

Tofler, I., & DiGeronimo, T. F. (2000). *Keeping your kids out front without kicking them from behind: How to nurture high-achieving athletes, scholars, and performing artists*. San Francisco: Jossey-Bass.

Tolson, G. H., & Cuyjet, M. J. (2007). Jazz and substance abuse: Road to creative genius or pathway to premature death. *International Journal of Law and Psychiatry, 30*, 530–538.

Torrance, E. P. (1966). *Torrance tests of creative thinking: Norms-technical manual*. Princeton, NJ: Personnel Press.

Torrance, E. P. (1974). *Torrance tests of creative thinking: Norms and technical manual*. Lexington, MA: Personnel Press/Ginn_Xerox.

Torrance, E. P. (1987). Teaching for creativity. In S. Isaksen (Ed.), *Frontiers of creativity research: Beyond the basics* (pp. 190–215). Buffalo, NY: Bearly Ltd.

Tranter, J. (1986). Interview with John Ashbery, New York City, 20 April 1985. *Scripsi, 4*(1), npg.

Treffinger, D., Isaksen, S. G., & Stead-Dorval, K. B. (2006). *Creative problem-solving: An introduction* (4th ed.). Waco, TX: Prufrock Press.

Trilling, B., & Fadel, C. (2009). *21st century skills: Learning for life in our times*. Englewood Cliffs,

NJ: Pearson.

Turner, F. (1985). *John Muir: Rediscovering America.* Cambridge, MA: Perseus Books.

Üusikylä, K., & Piirto, J. (2000). *Luovuus: Taitl löytää, rohkeus toteuttaa.* Jyväskylä, FI: WSOY.

Üusikylä, K., & Piirto, J. (2008d). Themes in the lives of Finnish orchestra conductors. In M. Laitinen & M.-L. Kainulainen (Eds.), *Musikaalisuuden ytimessä: In the heart of musicality. Juhlakirja Kai.Essays in honour of Kai Karma* (pp. 41–54). Helsinki, FI: Sibelius-Akatemia/ Musikkikasvatuksen osasto.

Venter, J. C. (2007). *A life decoded. My genome: My life.* New York: Penguin Group.

Walker, D. (Ed.). (1990). *Dear Nan: Letters of Emily Carr, Nan Chency, and Humphrey Toms.* Vancouver, BC: University of British Columbia Press.

Wallach, M. (1971). *The creativity-intelligence distinction.* New York: General Learning Press.

Wallach, M., & Kogan, N. (1965). *Modes of thinking in young children: A study of the creativity-intelligence distinction.* New York: Holt, Rinehart, & Winston, Inc.

Wallas, G. (1926). *The art of thought.* New York: Harcourt Brace Jovanovich.

Ward, T. B. (2001). Creative cognition, conceptual combination, and the creative writing of Stephen R. Donaldson. *American Psychologist, 56*(4), 350–354.

Weber, B. (2008, September 14). David Foster Wallace, influential writer, dies at 46. *New York Times.* http://www.nytimes.com/2008/09/15/books/15wallace.html.

Wells, D. H. (1996). Forced incubation. *Creativity Research Journal, 9*(1), 408–410.

Wiggins, J. (Ed.). (1996). *The five-factor model of personality.* New York: Guilford Press.

Winner, E. (1996). *Gifted children.* New York: Basic.

Zimmerman, B. J., Bandura, A., & Martinez-Pons, M. (1992). Self-motivation for academic attainment: The role of self-efficacy beliefs and personal goal setting. *American Educational Research Journal, 29*(3), 663–676.

Zinger, L. (2008). Educating for tolerance and compassion: Is there a place for meditation in the college classroom? *College Teaching Styles and Methods Journal, 4*(4), 25–28.

INDEX